The Sustaining Utterance

The Sustaining Utterance
Discourses on Chasidic Thought

ADIN STEINSALTZ

Edited and translated
by
Yehuda Hanegbi

JASON ARONSON INC.
Northvale, New Jersey
London

First Jason Aronson Inc. softcover edition—1996

10 9 8 7 6 5 4 3 2 1

Library of Congress Cataloging-in-Publication Data

  The sustaining utterance : discourses on Chasidic thought / Adin
Steinsaltz : edited and translated by Yehuda Hanegbi.
      p. cm.
  Transcription of lectures originally delivered in Hebrew by Rabbi
Adin Steinsaltz.
  ISBN 0-87668-845-8 (hardcover)
  ISBN 1-56821-997-0 (softcover)
  1. Shneur Zalman, of Lyady, 1745-1813. Sha'ar ha-yiḥud yeha.
-emunah 2. Hasidism. I. Hanegbi, Yehuda. II. Title.
BM198.S4863S74   1989
296.8'3322—dc20

                                                        89-6939

Manufactured in the United States of America. Jason Aronson Inc. offers books and cassettes. For information and catalog write to Jason Aronson Inc., 230 Livingston Street, Northvale, New Jersey 07647.

Contents

Acknowledgments

Warm thanks is due to Micha Taubman, our dear friend of many years, who made this translation possible.

Adin Steinsaltz
Yehuda Hanegbi

Translator's Preface

The Sustaining Utterance is a companion volume to The Long Shorter Way and, like it, is an English rendering of talks on Chasidic thought given by Rabbi Adin Steinsaltz in Jerusalem. More specifically, it is based on the second part (Shaar HaYichud VeHaEmunah) of the Collected Discourses of Rabbi Schneur Zalman of Liadi, the 18th-century founder of the Chabad movement.

Rabbi Steinsaltz gave more than one series of lectures on this book; besides the Thursday evening talks, there were the talks on the Israeli radio and elsewhere. In 1987, the first volume of these discourses was published in Hebrew. It contained a very full and well-edited compilation of all the versions of Rabbi Steinsaltz's commentary on the Shaar HaYichud VeHaEmunah. The present volume, in English, is an entirely different book and is based only on the transcripts of the Thursday evening talks.

One of the reasons, if not the main reason, why Rabbi Steinsaltz has returned to this little book, also called "Education of the Child" (notwithstanding its profundity), is that he feels it to be a valuable key to a certain school of Chasidic doctrine. To be sure, Jewish tradition has never indulged in

theological speculation to any appreciable extent, and
Chasidism was certainly averse to intellectual systems of any
sort. Nevertheless, in the text of the *Shaar HaYichud
VeHaEmunah* we are confronted with certain basic issues that
we can only consider theological, such as our knowledge of
God and the world. And Rabbi Steinsaltz's talks on the book,
given in the intimate atmosphere of a small group that met in
the basement of a Jerusalem synagogue, and ranging through
all the many forms of intellectual and spiritual explication,
anecdotes, and storytelling, association of ideas, and whatever
else a learned Jewish mind can bring to bear on the subject,
provides a new depth to our understanding of that side of
Chasidism. The editing had to omit many of the asides and the
pungent comments on current life, and of course, the English
language itself conveys a different flavor. The reader will have
to fill in. . . .

The chapter titles are the translator's own, but the numbers
of the chapters coincide with those of the Hebrew text of *Shaar
HaYichud VeHaEmunah*.

Foreword

The book known as the *Tanya* or "Collected Discourses" (*Likutei Amarim*) by Rabbi Schneur Zalman of Liadi differs from most Chasidic books by the fact of its having been conceived as a written work. The vast majority of books that have emerged from Chasidism were actually verbal teachings put down into writing by pupils. Even when the author of a teaching himself wrote, it was frequently done as though recording spoken words. There are a large number of books, in fact, that are not really writings as such, but rather "oral Torah," spoken material intended for further expansion and additional explanation.

The "Collected Discourses" is a classical Habad work composed of five books. The first book is entitled *Sefer HaBenonim* (Book of Intermediates) and is usually itself called the *Tanya*. The second book is *Shaar HaYichud VeHaEmunah* (Gate to Unity and Faith), also called *Chinuch Katan* (Education of the Child). An additional small work follows—*Igeret HaTeshuvah* (Letters of Repentance)—which, it would appear, is not quite complete. The fourth book consists of a collection of letters, whereas the fifth includes selections from the author's other writings. The work as a whole was not printed all at once. The first book came out separately, and then gradually the others were published at various intervals.

The main portions of the work as a whole are undoubtedly the first and second parts, namely, *Sefer HaBenonim* and *Chinuch Katan*. According to the testimony of pupils, the author intended to make the second part as large as the first, but for one reason or another, he never completed it as planned.

The two books are somehow juxtaposed, one against the other. The *Tanya* deals primarily with practical morality: Divine Service in the sense of love and fear of God, the inner conflicts of man, and ways of overcoming them and the like. The *Shaar HaYichud VeHaEmunah* is concerned with the fundamentals of faith.

The author of these profound works does not see himself as anything more than a compiler. This is not quite true, of course; the book is far too original to be considered a collection of other people's thoughts. Indeed, many works presuming to be original are far more in the nature of compilations than this one. His hesitation stems from the fact that at the early stages of Chasidism, written books were rather suspect; the movement was based on a living rabbi or teacher, called affectionately and with great awe, "Rebbe." A book could be seen as a repudiation of the need for a rebbe or live teacher, so that our author makes a point of declaring that his book is nothing more than a compilation of spoken teachings.

Among the sages who preceded and taught Rabbi Schneur Zalman, the most prominent were the Maggid of Mezritch and the son of the Maggid, Rabbi Avraham, who was called the "Malach" (Angel). The "Malach" left practically no writings at all and gave hardly any sermons or public talks, so that all that remains of his teachings is a little compilation of sayings called *Chesed Avraham*. The influence of the "Malach" on Rabbi Schneur Zalman was very profound—an emphasis on self-discipline and asceticism—which, although it was somewhat opposed to the main stream of Chasidic wholesomeness of divine worship, left its mark on Chabad thought. The third teacher of Rabbi Schneur Zalman was Rabbi Menachem Mendel of Vitebsk, who was officially the first spiritual heir of the Maggid. He remained the leader of the Chasidic movement even after he emigrated to the Land of Israel and was the last to be so accepted by all the movement's schools and various branches. Most of Menachem Mendel's sphere of influence was in Lithuania, all of which gradually became Chabad dominated. In any case, the Baal HaTanya (Rabbi Schneur Zalman) was always careful to indicate his debt to Rabbi Mendel.

The main distinction between the Baal HaTanya and his predecessors may be summed up by the production of the books of the *Tanya*. The others wrote or taught on a personal, inspired basis, relating always to specific issues and never really constructing an entire, intellectual system. In fact, those who are familiar with the history of Chasidism may be able to distinguish in the introduction certain undertones of the serious differences between Baal HaTanya and his contemporaries, who, opposed to any systemization of belief, were of the opinion that relations with God had to be kept free and unhampered by intellectual notions.

The additional name of "Education of the Child" to this work, *Shaar HaYichud VeHaEmunah*, is intended to indicate that the book is not supposed to be an exhaustive basis for Divine work or worship, but is rather a minimal set of instructions, the fundamentals necessary for a beginner, or a child. It does not attempt to lead one to an experience of spiritual heights. It is simply a manual of the theoretical aspects of Chabad Chasidism—the groundwork needed to maintain a religious poise. The core of the argument focuses on the meaning of the fundamental declaration, the *Shema* (Hear O Israel, The Lord is God, The Lord is One), at the heart of daily prayer. Since this is the basis for, and is always followed by, the statement, "Thou shalt love thy God, with all thy heart and all thy soul and all thy might . . ." it has to be treated as primary.

THE SEFIROT: THEIR STRUCTURE AND HUMAN CORRESPONDENCES

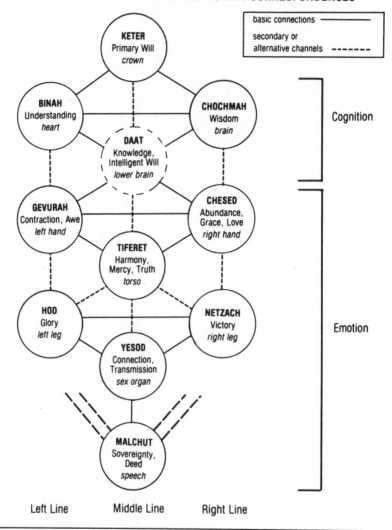

| basic connections | ——————— |
| secondary or alternative channels | - - - - - - |

KETER
Primary Will
crown

BINAH
Understanding
heart

CHOCHMAH
Wisdom
brain

DAAT
Knowledge,
Intelligent Will
lower brain

Cognition

GEVURAH
Contraction, Awe
left hand

CHESED
Abundance,
Grace, Love
right hand

TIFERET
Harmony,
Mercy, Truth
torso

HOD
Glory
left leg

NETZACH
Victory
right leg

YESOD
Connection,
Transmission
sex organ

MALCHUT
Sovereignty,
Deed
speech

Emotion

Left Line   Middle Line   Right Line

Malchut can be considered above as well as below the others, first as well as last. The broken lines from Malchut indicate that it connects itself to each of the Sefirot.

Daat and Keter are "interchangeable"; it is one or the other. Beyond cognition, there is no Daat; within cognition, Keter is not apprehendable.

This is only one version of the many possible diagrammatic representations of the Sefirot.

English translations of the names of the Sefirot: Keter, Crown; Chochmah, Wisdom; Binah, Understanding; Daat, Knowledge; Chesed, Grace; Gevurah, Strength; Tiferet, Splendor; Netzach, Victory; Hod, Glory; Yesod, Foundation; Malchut, Kingdom.

Introduction

Concerning the Education
of the Child

In the Book of Proverbs it is written, "Educate the Child according to his way; even when he is old he will not depart from it" (Proverbs 22:6). However, one should not educate the child to believe something that is correct only for one's childhood and has to be changed for more correct beliefs later on — "He'll understand when he grows up." On the contrary, the child has to be helped to understand in accordance with his capacities, and what he learns has to be correct, so that even when he grows up he won't find any discrepancies — it will still be correct.

Love is the root of doing good. Can we, however, distinguish between doing good and fulfillment of the positive precepts of the Torah? There is a general state of doing good, of love of God, that naturally brings a person who wishes to approach God to do the right thing. This state is not included in the positive precepts or commandments of the Torah; it belongs to a more general concept of love of God. Just as there are things a person refrains from doing out of sense of awe or fear of God and not because it is specifically forbidden, so, too, there is a general desire to do good that is expressed in the performance of positive precepts.

1

The education of the child is also one of the positive precepts and, therefore, an expression of the love of God. It is not only a matter of what is taught to one's children; it involves what one teaches to oneself, in the sense that one is in the category of a pupil or a child. There is also the mitzvah to educate oneself, which also comes from a love of God.

The question here is: How is it possible to command a person to love? As it has been said more than once, "Thou shalt love" is actually not a command or a precept to do something, but a conclusion to the preceding declaration: "The Lord is our God, the Lord is One." For once this declaration penetrates to one's consciousness, then the love of God follows naturally; it does not even have to be commanded. Indeed, this has been the subject of much discussion in Chasidism—the conviction that, intrinsically, love is that powerful fullness of emotion that comes of itself, that cannot help itself. The love of God is not something to be commanded or insisted upon. Here the author quotes a saying from the Bible (Deuteronomy 11:22), where the issue is pinpointed differently. The commandment is "to do it, to love the Lord your God." In other words, love of God is something one *does*.

In all the literature of Chabad, and in the *Tanya* itself, it is repeatedly emphasized that one should not rely on inspirations. One should be grateful for them, of course, but one should not build on gifts from Heaven, whether it be a matter of spiritual love or uplifting of the heart, whether it be awe or any other thought or feeling. A person has to work on himself; he has to work to know fear of God and he has to work to know love.

It may be in place to consider whether it is at all possible to use the expression "inducing" or "devising" love, for that which is essentially spontaneous, a matter of the heart. In reply to which, let us follow another thread of thought. It is said that it is impossible to counterfeit certain things; by its nature, the counterfeit is no longer the thing itself. In an essay attributed to one of the pupils of the Rabbi of Kotzk, it is asked, for instance, why it is that the seal of God is truth. And the answer is that a seal has to be something that cannot be counterfeited, and the Truth is precisely that, because as soon as one makes a counterfeit of Truth, it is no longer Truth. And this, then, is the same sort of question: How can one fashion love, since any contrived love is no longer love, but a product of the imagination? And a derivative question is: How can a person command his heart to think or feel one way or another?

The explanation is that there are two kinds of love of God. In one kind, the soul yearns for its Creator by its very nature, because it is a part of the Divine. It is an aspect of the yearning of a thing for its real self. It belongs to the very identity of the soul as soul and is not something that is imposed from outside the soul; indeed, as soon as the soul knows itself, this knowledge includes a love of God. The second kind is a love that comes from conscious effort and contemplation. For if the soul were only a spiritual being, without body, it could cling to God with complete abandon. But the soul of man is bound up with matter—even though matter is not in itself bad or blameworthy—and matter determines the limits of the soul's achievements, even its field of understanding and relationship. When, in childhood, a person first reaches some degree of understanding, this does not mean that he apprehends the spirituality of the self. It is merely that he has received some intimation of other things within the veiled perception of his body. Therefore, a person has to study until he learns to discriminate between the physical self and the rest of his being. For the distinction between matter and spirit is not a natural division; it emerges as a result of observation and introspection. Thus, physical desire, whether for the good or otherwise, is at first grasped by man as the desire of his very self. Only afterward is there room for discrimination: What do I really want? What is merely a reflex action and what is an inner need? All these are matters for investigation and discussion; they issue from the fact that the body and the soul grow together out of the one cradle, and for a long time, the soul does not know the world or itself except through the instruments of its physical shell.

If we may use an old, not so agreeable image, we may picture the metempsychosis or passage of the soul through animal and human forms, until the soul learns that it does not have to function according to the pattern of an animal. Man is brought up in terms of animal selfhood because the human body, no matter how developed, is that of an animal. Which also explains man's limitations, incidentally, even the restrictions of his intellectual qualities. In order to discover the fact that he is a human being, something of an entirely different essence, he has to separate the vessel from its contents, and he has to learn to see the world with other eyes, not through his ordinary implements of vision. Therefore, it is said that the soul has first to overcome physical matter, to overcome it in the same sense of overcoming the first level of life, where matter rules supreme. Afterward, it is not enough that the soul becomes stronger—the physical nature has to be subjugated and used. For the soul, no matter how liberated it is, has to function physically through the body and has to think through the physical brain. Not only the body as such, but even the brain, or the mind, has to be transformed into an instrument.

In the struggle between body and soul, the question to be decided is not only who is stronger, but who will rule over the other. At first there is the overcoming of the other, the taming, whereupon the body becomes an instrument for the soul, and the body ceases to act on its own wishes. To use an example, the soul may be likened to a horseman, or perhaps, to go further, to a person driving a car who, not being familiar with the way the engine works, may imagine that it operates by itself, that is to say, in accordance with the laws of its own structure. Only after a long period of using the car does a person begin to realize that it is an extension of himself and that it doesn't have a will of its own nor is it likely to rebel against him. In short, only when the body is completely controlled does the soul feel free, because so long as the soul has to clench the reins tightly and struggle against the body, it cannot feel inspired or exhilarated. The soul strives and labors to extricate itself. Only when it reaches a degree of genuine control over matter does it "blaze forth." Thus released and, in this sense, pure, it can do as it pleases. Which is what is meant by the saying that he who truly sees this world as it is in his lifetime is privileged to possess the next world. For the difference between the next world and this world is not one of place, but in the power of the soul—the extent to which the soul can be free. If a person reaches that stage wherein the soul rules the body as though the body doesn't exist any more as something with a desire of its own, then his soul exists here in the same way as it would in Paradise. As the book *Chinuch Katan* says: "Then will the love of God flare and blaze with a flame that ascends of its own accord, and (the soul) will rejoice and exult in God its maker and will delight in Him with wonderous bliss."

The state of Great Love (Ahavah Rabbah) is a high level of love, being self-sustaining and free of the need for anything to support it or guide it. To achieve it, a person's physical being has to be purified very much. That is one requirement. The other is the need to become immersed in Torah and good deeds. The involvement here in Torah is not only for the sake of the Torah, but in order to attain a Higher Soul (Neshamah), a category of spiritual being that is higher than Spirit (Ruach) and Vital Soul (Nefesh). These are the three levels of growth in the realm of spiritual being, and the attainment of the highest level, of Neshamah, is the result of realizing Torah and mitzvot.

The Higher Soul is not easily achieved. At first the body has to be dealt with and eliminated as an obstacle; secondly, a person has to have enough natural drive to be able to become enthusiastic and full of a certain alacrity for God. An illustration, even if an extreme contrast, is the way the spontaneous explosion of radioactive material takes place as a result of a high degree of purity and a certain accumulation of material. In other words, it is not enough for a person to be faultless in virtue; his soul has to possess such a high accumulation of spiritual energy that the kindling occurs of itself, spontaneously. It depends then on a special higher aspect of Soul, and not everyone can attain to it. A person who is merely on the level of Nefesh (Vital Soul), for example, cannot reach this illuminated state of inner being. Altogether few people are ever so privileged, and for most, it leads to frustration and subsequent questioning of one's worth. It may even be said that its attainment defines the Tzadik, who is a superior person.

For most people the Great Love (Ahavah Rabbah) is not attainable, and they have to develop the other kind of love, Ahavat Olam (love that comes out of the world). One must therefore learn to engage in profound contemplation in the depths of the heart. To do so is, first of all, an intellectual act; to contemplate is connected with what one knows. A person may be aware of, or know about, spiritual things in a vague sort of way; but to engage in deep contemplation is connected with knowing in a more profound sense. It is a matter of having a clear intellectual grasp of all the aspects of the object of one's contemplation and not just having an impression of the thing. Furthermore, the contemplation has to be profound, in the "depths of the heart." For clearly it is not enough for it to be confined to the intellect. And in the heart of every Jew the love of God is an innate reality. Of course, the love of God is potentially in the heart of every human being, but there is another (or additional) love of God that is specifically derived from the fact that a person is a Jew. This is connected with the saying, "I am the Lord your God who took you out of the Land of Egypt. . . ." which refers also to the quality of readiness to respond in the heart of every Jew, even if he is not a Tzadik. The fact that someone is of Israel makes him susceptible to spiritual realities; he is at least potentially able, after a certain amount of suitable effort, to receive certain fruits.

Of course, there is a general, human way for all men, which is primary: "That He is our very life" (Deuteronomy 30:20). And when a person contemplates this truth that He is our very life, then the thought takes us beyond the fact of His greatness to the core of one's own self. One begins to realize the "I" who is at the heart of the matter of love. Even love of oneself requires this recognition; it is the starting point of an individual's discovery of his own personality. Beyond that, there is the deeper awareness of knowing the self within, the I, the one who realizes that God is that Self of the self. Thus, when we say, "He is our life," the intention here is not that He is the giver of life, but that He Himself is our life. When I search for the I in the body, I find the I of the soul; when I search for the I of the soul, I find the I of the Divine.

Therefore, one must meditate well and one must contemplate in the depths of the heart. The two are both necessary. First one must come to terms with the concept of the absolute identity between the self of all the grades of one's being.

Beyond all this, man discovers God in the ultimate Self. For which, as has been said, one needs a concentrated effort of both mind and body. It is not enough for a person to give it his outer attention, or to relate to it as an idea and nothing more. Even as an idea it has to be clear and has to be worked out until the person knows it well. For instance, and even today the example holds, when I wish to grasp the idea that the earth is round, it is not so difficult when I consider it abstractly and logically; but when I have to consider that I am now up or above, and there are people opposite who are nevertheless not standing on their heads, a certain amount of confusion enters. For it is hard to make a switch in orientation and to see any other system of coordinates outside of one's own. How much more difficult is this in regard to the concept of God, when I have to transcend the grasp of myself. Beyond me and below me there is a me who is God.

"And just as one loves his soul and his life, so he will love God when he will meditate and reflect in his heart that God is his true soul and actual life." Or, if we wish to say it in more forthright terms, there is a sort of development of self-love, whereby a certain elementary love of oneself reaches ever higher and deeper levels of existence beyond the physical and the vital. The idea is connected with the view of Chabad Chasidism on the education of the child, which does not place so much emphasis on inspiration, enthusiasm, and sudden revelation. Agreed, such lofty experiences are possible, and certainly desirable, but one should take into consideration that they are not very common. In practice, there is another way, and that is the way of faith and spiritual consistency, which is essentially a matter of education. That is, it is a way based on the transmission and development of concepts. One acquires a concept and proceeds further step by step. One of the great rabbis of the Chabad movement, the Rashab, who died in Russia in 1920, used to say that man sins, and when he is brought before the Heavenly court, he is judged twice. First, he is asked why he did not keep the Commandments and refrain from transgression; second, if he had to transgress, why could he not have chosen at least to do something beautiful? And the sinner is adjudged for the ugliness of his deeds as well as for their wrongness. What is indicated here is a process of spiritual education from satisfaction to satisfaction, from love of the crudest sort to the most refined, to the level of the love of God. In this sense, the love of God is, as was once said by a certain Tzadik, a lust like any other appetite, except that in order to satisfy this particular passion, one has first to shatter all the other lusts. As a lust, Divine love is a form of egoism, even if it is a passion that a person seeks to satisfy within himself. It is egoism in that one does not negate oneself; one only probes and penetrates deeper into oneself. And it is a gradual and difficult route in the course of which the soul is refined – the awareness of the self becomes ever more subtle and inward – and only toward the end do works expressing the nature of this newly discovered soul become paramount.

It is written, "(You are) my soul; I long for you in the night" (Isaiah 26:9). Thus God is my soul. This idea is inherent in other phrases defining God as "the rock of my heart" or "my eye." All of which is intended to express the essential inwardness of the relationship; it is not a matter of reaching a turning point or climax but rather a going deeper and deeper, depending on the training of the mind and education of the soul. Which is why it is necessary for the ordinary person to learn the theory. The complete Tzadik doesn't have to learn theory because for him the experience comes of itself; it is the person who is not a complete Tzadik who has to learn technique or theory in order to know how to relate the self to God.

This is one level of love – a general kind, that of common humanity. And this grade, of "He is our life," is attainable by all men. But there is a more explicit kind of love – when one begins to understand God's greatness in detail, after analyzing and breaking it down to particulars, so that a certain clarity and wonder emerge, as well as a better idea of size and proportion. True, there is a limit to what a human being can reach in terms of intellectual abstraction, and, as it has been said, this limit is the frontier of one's humanity. As a person develops, he strives to get beyond this frontier of his mind and in doing so achieves more in the realm of refined abstraction. The question is: How does a person know what is beyond his intellect? But, just as one can see, for instance, no further than the horizon and yet know that there is something beyond it, so one can perceive with the intelligence a little of what is beyond, if only in terms of a more profound comprehension of distances. At which point one will be able to "contemplate God's great and wonderous love to us" as manifested by His descent to Egypt, in order to save us from the "crucible of iron" (Jeremiah 11:4).

Traditionally, then, God's great love to us, to Israel in particular, is shown by the descent to Egypt. He went down to Egypt, not only because of Israel's being there physically, but also because the Children of Israel were becoming like the Egyptians, copying and resembling them. The "crucible of iron" is, in this context, the extreme of the hot-bed of evil, which is called the gates of pollution. And God descends to the gates of pollution of Egypt to extricate the souls of Israel from the iron crucible. "To bring us close to Him and to bind us to His very name, and He and His name are one" (*Zohar* II:90b). Which means that although we were at the point of utmost degradation when God brought us forth, He called us by His Name and let us cling to Him. There is no difference in this sense between God and His Name.

From which it may be determined that the Exodus from Egypt is not only a manifestation of the power of God, but also, and more profoundly, it expresses the love of God. Only when the greatness of God is realized can one understand what it means for Him to go down to Egypt and take us out from there. There is a story of a man who had committed a sin. He came to one of the Tzadikim and asked for remission, for repentance. He thought that, as was customary, he would be given certain penances and fasts to perform, but the teacher told him that he did not wish to impose any ascetic practices on him. Instead, he made the man sit with him every day and study, irrespective of subject matter. They pored over those items dealing with the greatness of the Creator and those belonging to the degradation of sin. Until finally the man reached such a level of contrition and self-dislike that the others in the group took pity on him and made the teacher release him to go off and fast a bit and rest from these torments. There are many other parables in this vein. One of them is that a foolish peasant once insulted the king, not knowing what he was doing. He had to be brought to the royal palace and be shown the king in all his greatness before he understood the enormity of his offense. Which is to say that to realize something of the vast distance between God and man enables us to catch a glimpse of the nature of His love for us. Thus, the Exodus from Egypt is an expression of Divine love, being God's voluntary descent from the highest to the lowest; the frequent emphasis of this in the prayers is always directed to the love this invokes.

It is said that just as in water the face of man is reflected, so does the heart of man reflect that of another. The feelings of another person to me make me feel that way to him. I respond likewise, naturally, automatically. And the more I understand the love of the other toward me, the less I can withstand it, the less indifferent I can be. In another context it is explained that this is the real difficulty in the phenomenon of bribery; every kind of bribe, even flattery, has an influence beyond the weight of the action itself. For there is a distinctive gesture that cannot be resisted. One can wipe it out intellectually, but one cannot erase the natural reaction. That responsiveness is, in a way, connected with our very physical existence, so that, in answer to the question, "How does one reach the love of God?" one simply has to try to understand the love of God for us; when one can grasp something of that, there is awakened the reaction of our love for God.

Apparently, it is not merely a matter of gratitude; indeed, there is very little mention of the need to be grateful for God's taking me out of Egypt. The emphasis is rather on the idea that I should feel something of God's love for me. And only when I feel this love of God for me can I reciprocate with a similar feeling; something is awakened in me and the more intense my emotions and understanding, the more complete and sincere is my response.

Divine love is generated by preparing the groundwork of the inner soul structure. The spontaneous love that flows of itself is a rare capacity that belongs to those special individuals who have shattered the common fabric and laws of human nature. But most individuals, who are still very human, have not broken through to anything else, and they have to make an effort to develop that which is within the scale of the human. Thus, to experience Divine love, most men have to work

toward it, to develop it. Building on a firm intellectual infra-
structure, it is possible to attain a genuine emotional relationship with God, but this, in turn, is possible only on the basis of
faith, or at least on a reliable standard of measure, such as is
afforded by tradition.

~~~~~~

One "can devote one's heart and mind to matters that
stimulate love," but it is impossible to order a person to love
God with the love that must come of itself. And it is not only
the love that comes of itself that cannot be ordered or commanded; since it is an essentially free expression outside the
realm of willed action, even more so is it impossible to summon
that love which is a gift of God to man. The latter cannot even
be considered a part of Divine worship; it is more in the nature
of the reward—such love is actually the compensation of
devotion. If so, what is true of the next world? In the world to
come, the soul delights in the radiance of the *Shechinah* or in
some other manner rejoices in the love of God and the fear of
God. On the other hand, the one who has refined his physical
being, purified the substance of his life to the utmost, who has
arrived at the maximum of his capacities in Torah and good
deeds and has achieved a Higher Soul—what more does he
need to be in the next world? For the whole matter of the next
world is not a matter of a place to which one must go; it is a
level of being that one must attain. Therefore, this level of love
is not connected with what a person can be commanded to
perform; it simply follows from what a person actually is.

The purpose of all this meditation on God's love is to bring
us back to the question of education and the verse, "For a
Tzadik falls seven times and rises again" (Proverbs 24:16). The
first, rather obvious point made here is that the Tzadik, like
other types of men, is not immune to weakness and failure.
Since the way is a human way, it is strewn with obstacles and
pitfalls.

The other, more subtle point is that this very falling of the
Tzadik (sage) is part of his work. To be sure, one may also
expect the sage to be able to avoid the pitfalls of ordinary
mortals and to pursue a relatively smooth path, with only

occasional collapse. But to make the falling an integral part of the way of the Tzadik is the very contrary approach, an attitude in which the smooth, easy path is somewhat suspect. The falling and the rising and the falling again are indications of the unending conflict within. This is important to begin with, because sometimes a person may feel that his failure or decline is a sign of something essentially wrong. Whereas, as it is stated here and elsewhere, to fall is no sign of failure, but rather that one is making progress, that something essential is alive within one, something which, if it is lacking, makes progress impossible and invites the Angel of Death.

There are stories to this effect, like the one of Rabbi Bunim of P'shisha, who said that a person should see himself as though his head were resting on the block and the "evil impulse" were standing over him, axe in hand, ready to chop off his head, and that this is the way a person has to relate to the matter of temptation and wrong action. One of the pupils of the Rabbi asked, "And what about someone who does not see things that way?" To which Rabbi Bunim answered, "That's a sign that the evil impulse has already lopped off his head." In short, the person who has no doubts and failures may be suspected of having already experienced the great fall, after which one is no longer sensitive to the process of decline. There is also the saying of the Baal Shem Tov concerning the verse, "And I shall surely hide my countenance . . ." (Deuteronomy 31:18), whose emphasis (the word "surely") serves to show that the hiddenness itself will be hidden. When people do not know that the Divine countenance is turned away from them, the hiddenness is that much greater. For so long as a person knows that God's face is turned away from him, he may still be saved and be raised up within the human rhythm of rise and fall; but when he does not know it, then the fall is final.

The way of the Tzadik, therefore, is to fall seven times and rise. "Especially since man is called 'mobile' and not 'static'!" The "static," or standing ones, are the angels, being unchanging in their inner being, whereas the human Tzadik is mobile, walking among these standing ones, his soul progressing always and moving on to a higher level of being. For even if he reaches the level of the angel Michael he is not permitted, being a human being, to remain at this level; he has to become more than the archangel. He has to advance from victory to victory and can never rest on his laurels. Man is, therefore, destined to change and rise up as part of his human condition. He may also decline and fall; there is no middle way in which he can remain motionless.

Moreover, when a person passes from one level to another, there is an increased danger of falling. He is no longer secure in the previous level, and can easily fall before he gains a hold in the next level. This is true, of course, for every change in condition or of level of existence. For instance, when entering the water to swim, there is a moment when one has to lose balance, disconnect from secure contact with the ground, and be neither walking nor floating. Transition thus always involves imbalance and danger; it is in passing that one may collapse and lose all. The purpose of the quoted exhortation is to keep a person from falling too much.

Thus, too, if someone who is learning some skill—either manual or intellectual—is put into a situation where there is a real difference of approach to the subject, it seems fairly necessary to advise the person to forget all that he had learned previously, because it would only serve to confuse him. He cannot progress to a higher level of performance without forgetting, letting go of what he already knows. So that those people, for example, who are intrinsically unable to forget are also those who find it hard to progress. The passage from one level to another demands a sort of leap, an abandoning of all that was solid ground. It is a basic feature of human progress, resting on the principle that the interval between points or fields comprises a mode of nothingness, and one cannot proceed from one point to another without losing one's previous balance, even if only for the briefest moment. There is the story of Rabbi Zeira of Babylonia, who came to Palestine and wanted to study the Jerusalem Talmud. To do so, he underwent a hundred fasts in order to forget the Babylonian Talmud. But what was he left with? He did indeed forget the Babylonian Talmud. Before he managed to learn the Jerusalem Talmud, was he an ignorant boor? It is, of course, far more complex. The decline, as in such a case, is relative. One forgets a category of knowledge in order to be able to learn something of another kind. Indeed, it is not an uncommon problem: How much should one forget? Confusion and disturbance may result from holding on to something when it is no longer needed. And this desire to retain the hard-won knowledge and at the same time to venture forth into something new and rise to a higher level may well lead to an impasse. At the same time, one cannot change that which transpired in the soul. A person who has worked on himself and has reached a certain level of being cannot lose that which was gained, even if at a certain moment it slips away from conscious awareness. There remains an impression on the soul that cannot be wiped out.

The Chasidic disciples of Kotzk used to be renowned for their undisciplined defiance of all set times and order; they used to pray with such great fervor and inwardness that their morning prayers would extend into the afternoon, and evening prayers into the morning, and they had little regard for outer convention. But when the leader of the Gur sect took over, a relatively young man, truthspeaking and straight, he decided that prayers were to be held at fixed times. At first, it was thought that such a sharp change would arouse serious opposition; but it turned out otherwise. The Chasidim of Kotzk, who all their lives had lived in a certain atmosphere of timelessness, were able to accept the new edict; eight o'clock means precisely eight. And this was their power to progress— their ability to abandon the good and even valuable in their customary way, and to forget it.

This brings us back to the educational skill that will guide a person all his life. This way of Divine service is a complicated path with many rises and declines, and every man falls. If a person does not have a good basis to begin with, he is that much more prone to total failure. Therefore, the main thing is the foundation, that which is irrefutable and beyond doubt, being solidly entrenched in the soul, and which, even when passing from one level to another, is not shaken. One has to try to reach a level of such certainty and security that risks can be taken in pursuing some of the ways of the Tzadikim, with their attendant danger of falls. When such a basis has been established, one may proceed further.

All of which is an explanation for, or an introduction to, the subject of faith. True, every person has to reach his own comprehension of this matter, and that which is taught is never sufficient. Why, then, should one try to teach? The answer is that there has to be a certain minimum that is the basis, a firm foundation that can support a human being; otherwise, he falls and cannot rise again. For even the best of men fall, as shown by the inclusion in the Chabad prayer book of a letter by Baal HaTanya to his friend, Rabbi Levi Yitzchak of Berditchev, who experienced a fall and loss of all his enthusiasm and all the intense vigor of his prayer, so that he used to sit and pray like an ordinary man, finish quickly, and go about his business. In this letter, it is clear from the way it is formulated that Rabbi Levi Yitzchak desperately wishes to extricate himself from this condition, either by ascetic practices or some other drastic measure. Another very moving testimony is that of the Rabbi of Buchach, who wrote that one of his most difficult problems, one that brought on a severe crisis, was how to go from the world of learning to the world of Chasidism. He says that there used to be times when he could not hold on to one or the other, and he suffered agonies until, with the help of his teachers, he found a way of retaining a firm grasp on both worlds. We have here cases of the disruption that occurs when a person passes from one world to another, especially at the moment when he loses the secure contact with the previous world. Being in the middle and deprived of support, his spirit is tormented within him.

1

The Letters of the Ten Utterances

The Baal Shem Tov explains the Divine Word, not as a metaphor, but as possessing specific actuality. This speech of God, which created the heavens, is actually present in the heavens; the very syllables and the letters of "Let there be a firmament" uphold the heavens and make it possible for the heavens to exist. It is not only something that occurred in the past, but is something that is taking place all the time; God speaks always. When a man speaks, his words, as definite substances, fade into nothingness. The Words of God remain forever. We comprehend this metaphorically, as though to illustrate that Divine speech makes things happen. But it is not only that which is manifested that endures, but also the very words and letters continue to exist.

Let us endeavor to imagine that Divine speech is not a transient phenomenon, but a continuous one, repeating itself over and over. As though—and one must realize that this is only an illustration—one were to switch on an electric light. In alternating currents, such as we use here for ordinary purposes, the electric current goes back and forth all the time. One may thus see the Creation of the world as such a switching on

16

of a current. What is done by throwing a switch is not a completed action; it only releases a continuous and repeated movement of energy that remains dependent on the source. Divine speech is thus eternal in manifestation and is continually renewed. It is the formation of a pattern that endures as a dynamic interaction. The Baal Shem Tov once explained, in another context, how this was true of the Revelation of the Torah on Mount Sinai. It was a speaking of the Eternal Word in the sense, too, that it is being eternally spoken. There has not been any ceasing of this Divine speech; it is we who have ceased to listen. At the confrontation of Sinai, not only was that said which was said, but it was granted us that our ears be opened to hear what was being said. And the Baal Shem Tov concludes by saying that anyone can be privileged to stand on Mount Sinai and hear the Torah at any moment in his life. The confrontation at Mount Sinai is unique and single, not because the word of God has ceased to be spoken, but because we do not let our ears remain open to hear it.

Therefore, we read, "If the letters of the ten utterances by which the earth was created during the six days of creation were to depart from it (but) for an instant, God forbid, it would revert to naught and absolute nothingness, exactly as before the six days of creation." By which it is reiterated that the departing of the letters is not only a matter of loss of life force or of some other deprivation. If the Divine speech ceases, the result is a reverting to nonbeing. The letters of this Divine utterance did not create the things of the world; they are the very substance of things.

Here it would be helpful perhaps to bring another example—and again it has to be understood only as an illustration and not as any sort of description. When in our modern view of the world we speak of matter, it is only in very general and relative terms that we recognize it as solid and inert. An object like a table is composed of constantly moving particles whose physical solidity is rather questionable. Electrons may actually be apprehended as concentrated points of energy waves. In short, even within the realm of the physical world we are caught in a net of unreality; that which seems solid is not really so. It is not a matter of our senses deceiving us; the senses give a straightforward enough projection of things as they appear to be and as they are meant to be. What is being said by the teacher is that all matter, even that which appears to us real and solid, derives its existence from the Divine word.

Thus, even in earth or water there is spiritual essence. The stone has more of a soul, in a way, than the human body because it is more completely dominated by the soul-of-the-stone, while man has more soul than the stone, because he has more independent essence. The soul-of-the-stone is the Divine, form-giving force that substantiates the stone; if this Divine force should depart from the stone, there is no stone at all. When the soul of man departs from his body, the body continues to exist for a short while. To remove the soul of the stone is like switching off the electric current; there is no more light and all is extinct.

We are confronted with the very human problem based on the fact that the soul and the body are not identical. Were the soul to so dominate the human being that life would express only the soul, then the human being would disappear as soon as the soul left. Which, incidentally, is connected with the matter of sin and repentance. For if a person sinned in such a way that his punishment is to be cut off, then his soul would be consumed and the person would cease to exist. The whole point of repentance is that a human being does, somehow, continue to exist, at least certain remnants do, in order to be able to make amends. In other words, human beings have, in this sense, a double life; there is the life of the body and the life of the soul. And it is this that makes for problems in the spiritual life, because the body has its own desires; it does not merely express the desires of the soul. For instance: I decide to put my hand into the fire and I can observe how the body protests.

This is what happens in the relations between body and soul in man. But inert matter has no such soul; there is no conflict of desires. The soul of an object is the essence of its physicality. That which we know as the physical stone is a physical projection of the letters of the Divine speech that gives the stone its being. Just as the spatial dimensions characteristic of matter are projections of the movement and arrangements of molecules, so is all that we know as the world a result of Divine utterance, which appears as stone, flower, or anything.

We read that "although the name 'stone' is not mentioned in the Ten Utterances recorded in the Torah, nevertheless life-force flows to the stone through combinations and substitutions of the letters that are transposed in the 231 gates." This endeavors to explain the relation between that which is divinely spoken and the infinite detail that is created thereby. When, for instance, it is written, "God said 'Let there be a firmament,' " the words we read are some human version of that which God said. The inconceivable that is spoken by the Divine is translated in two ways. First it is translated by the firmament itself (in all its details). Second it is translated into that which is written in the Torah.

To use an example, we may conceive sound waves as being received and registered either by a magnetic tape or by a phonograph record. The magnetic tape will convert them into some sort of electromagnetic signals; the record will convert them into grooves on the plastic material. These are two different translations of the sound waves that, when the sound is projected, are translated back into the same thing. Now— sound waves, in themselves, are neither a magnetic signal on tape nor grooves in a record. When I wish to show them to anyone, I have to resort to one or another of the conversions or translations. In this sense, the letters of the Divine speech as manifested by the firmament are a different version, or another translation, of the same thing that is written in the Torah. Although one realizes that they are identical, one has to be aware of the fact that they are both humanized projections, that is, capable of being received and understood by man through his limited faculties. Thus, too, there are gifted persons who can look at a page of musical notes and not only sing them, but read them with pleasure as another reads a book and sometimes with even greater enjoyment than if they were to hear a concert rendering of the piece. This is more or less similar to what one may say of a great soul who reads the Torah—he hears the word of God in it, and it is for him a very different thing than for the one who reads logical sentences. Indeed, it may be said that the same thing holds true for any kind of reacting to the world; reception depends on one's capacities. There is the famous story of the Baal HaTanya who, a short time before his death, called his grandson, later known as the Tzemach Tzedek, and asked him, "What do you see?" The boy replied that he saw the ordinary things of a house. "And I," said the old man, "see only the word of God." There is a level, then, at which a person ceases to see – when he becomes aware of the thing itself rather than what is apparent from its modes of projections.

The letters, and the words of Torah we make of them, are translations into a specific mode of communication, a contrivance called writing. On the other hand, every letter is a Divine force, and therefore these letters cannot appear to us directly as they are; moreover, there are also different combinations of letters. The same letters combine, not only in the form of words, but also in various other ways, circles within circles, from one level of meaning to higher levels, from essence to essence; and within these circles there are various revelations of the same thing.

The letters thus combine in various permutations until we get the word "stone." Which is only partly to explain that the Ten Utterances contain all the letters – for the combination is not an accidental one resulting from chance groupings of the letters: it is a very definite union of three specific letters that belong to the earth. The word "stone" does not have any of the "letters" of "heaven" in it, but rather the three earthly letters it needs to undergo its various transmutations. Examples from modern chemistry may help us grasp the point. When working with chemical formulas, it makes a considerable difference if I replace any one letter by another. In modern organic chemistry, it is important even to designate direction, whether it is left or right – just as there are certain words, in Hebrew, composed of three letters, the third the same as the first, which have two distinct meanings depending on which "direction" they are read.

Hence, every created object has its own form, its own special essence, which is connected with the letters that formed it; and these letters are a certain expression of the Ten Utterances. When the Ten Utterances express themselves in another realm, and on another level, it does not manifest in the form of a stone. In a higher world, these Ten Utterances have another meaning; only as they are transmuted and descend to this world do they assume the meaning they have for us. It might be in place here to observe that in almost every domain these divisions are necessary and useful. For in the complex jumble of almost all compounded things in the world, an individual thing is defined by "number," i.e., by size and the level occupied by the formula of its composition, and so on. In integral calculus there is a similar problem, of taking a formula and raising it to a certain power, the fourth or fifth or whatever, by which it undergoes a certain transmutation that gives the result another meaning. All of which is only a reflection of a part of the problem we are dealing with here, in which the levels are not raised to the fourth or fifth power or even to the hundredth power, but to the millionth, in which the levels expand and grow in all directions. So that the basic formula of the Ten Utterances is broken up into a vast number of worlds in each of which there are different instructions given, the Divine forces manifest differently so that every object and detail, not only the stone as rock fragment, but every particle of substance in the universe no matter where, derives its special being from a particular life-force. And this Divine speech, the special combination of letters that supports the being of this particle, is single and unique, and the particle next to it is another, with another history and another essence and another name.

Indeed, it is afterward mentioned that every single thing has its own name, even the smallest and most inconspicuous item. So that, incidentally, it is said that when parents give their child a name, thinking that they know exactly why they are doing so, the truth is that they don't know why they are choosing it. And if they make a mistake and give a wrong name, the child will afterward change it because the name is not his correct one. This attempt to define who one is spills over into the identity of every soul, which also has an appropriate name, a specific formula. It is so for every star in the sky, too, each one with its name: "He counts the number of the stars; He calls them all by their names . . ." (Psalm 147:4). On the other hand, there are things that, like points on a topo-graphical map, can be sufficiently defined by their coordinates, the intersection of latitude and longitude. And if there are three dimensions, the appropriate numbers of each provide suffi-cient information to define it. Now, let us imagine something with thousands of dimensions, or even millions, each one requiring its own number or name, in order to express the formula of its being that is its animating power, its life-force. It is from this that the thing draws sustenance and that explains the essence of its soul, even if it is a stone, which does not mean, of course, that if I speak to a stone the stone will understand me, but rather that everything created out of Divine speech necessarily has a sort of soul of its own.

Interestingly, the great sage, the Maharal, also speaks of this, in his own terms, without Kabbalistic overtones, saying that miracle is based on the fact that the human being who performs a miracle sees the Divine speech in the world more clearly than he sees the material substance of the world, and Divine speech is, to a degree, given to manipulation by the one who compre-hends it. That is to say, the one who realizes that there is no table here has gone beyond the table, while for the one who does not see this, the table remains a table. It seems to be a question then: Where am I in terms of things? What is my relation to the objects of the world? Such as, for instance, the miracle that everyone can perform—walking on what is called the waters of the lake, when it is frozen over. The problem, then, is how I can relate to things in their changing state, and to what extent I am able to expand my relations to a static, immobile condition. From this point of view, the miracle is a matter of shifting things about a little in the world.

Incidentally, the matter of repentance is also a similar prob-lem. By repentance, I reach a certain level, by virtue of which I change something—and the whole point of repentance is that it alters some genuine reality in the world. Only when a person reaches such a level can he be said to atone. The world and its objects seem to be fixed only because we are all suspended within the same dimension. The man who is able to act on things in a different dimension, such as that of the microscopic world or of nuclear physics, does not feel that there is any difference between solid matter and any other kind of matter.

As far as electrons are concerned, it is all the same, whether they go through gases or through solid metal. We may add that also in our ordinary existence we live on a number of levels, and when I am on a certain level, then for something to have a distinguishable form on another level, it is sufficient for it to appear to be so. So that what is spiritual and what is physical depends on the relation I have, from my vantage point, to the things concerned.

2

Life and Providence

The Ten Utterances are very inclusive forces creating whole worlds and general essences. Only as a result of combinations, descents, replacements, and substitutions of their letters, from level to level, is it possible, finally, to reach a specific creation, such as a star, a human being, a blade of grass, and the like.

The question is asked whether that would be the name of the particular thing. To be sure, the name serves not only as a means of distinguishing things, but as a formula defining the essence of the thing. Thus, the name, which is the formula of something, becomes that by which it is called in the Holy Tongue, which in turn becomes a vessel, concentrating in its letters the life force of the object.

Indeed, this was one of the reasons for the opposition to modern Hebrew. It wasn't a matter of the secular usage of the Holy Tongue; after all, one can also use biblical Hebrew to express all sorts of vulgar banalities. It was not the misuse of the language, then, that aroused concern, but the creation of new names, new words. This was considered an act of primordial creation and not to be done artificially, without proper knowledge. And in this sense Hebrew is no longer purely a holy language, because there is no sacred relation between the thing and its name. The name we humans give to an object is often a product of whim, unrelated to its real essence.

In any event, the intention here is that the name of a thing is its basic formula, and when this is not complete in some way, even in the spelling or punctuation, most certainly in the level of its distinctiveness, the object is that much less existent.

The essential point is that the things in the world exist by virtue of the fact that the Divine speech continues to be spoken in them. The Divine speech is not a unique phenomenon; it is a continuous action, a process, of what is sometimes known as the "two hundred and thirty-one gates" (the possible combinations of each of the twenty-two letters of the Hebrew alphabet with one another), interrelating and interweaving in myriads of ramifications, echoing and reverberating from form to form. So that the speech and the echo of this speech are that which create the world. The Divine speech sustains the heavens and the earth, and when the speaking stops, heaven and earth cease to exist.

Divine Providence is not a general expression for a total state of affairs; it is something very definite that belongs to every created thing in the universe. Not only does Providence manifest on a grand scale; it is just as evident in the most insignificant event that occurs to a blade of grass, to a worm. It is all connected, of course, with the power of the letters, signs, and symbols of the Torah—which, incidentally, have always been greatly misunderstood.

The error stems from an incorrect comparison with the human concept of creating or making. It is stated that God made the heaven and the earth, and we say that man also makes things. The fundamental problem, then, concerns the concept of Creation, of making the world. In philosophical thought known as "Deism," the Creator makes the world and leaves it to go by itself. To be sure, even in the Bible there are a few instances when God seems to have abandoned the world to its own devices. However, this is not the problem here, nor whether it is blasphemy or not, because the whole image of a world abandoned by its Creator is based on a false analogy. The difference between human creativity and Divine creativity is not a matter of who is doing the creating, but of the essence of the created thing and the act of creation.

For example—let us take a living creature that has already matured and been made whole. At the same time, the body has to renew itself continuously; there has to be ever additional creation for the body to remain alive. This points to the difference between the completion of a design and the process of creation. The process of creation is continuous; at the same time it follows a pattern of growth, of individual completion and disintegration. The world is sustained by the continuous "saying" of the same Ten Utterances forever. The work of man is actually secondary and external; he merely alters the shape of the original substance, whereas the Divine action is that of making something come into being where nothing at all existed.

When one is working with nature it is not necessary to keep a strong hold of the thing being created; one may rely on a system of natural forces to bring about certain developments in the creative process. On the other hand, when one operates against nature, it is necessary to be incessantly active and alert in order to make certain things happen. Thus, if a ball is rolled on a level surface, a little push is enough to set it in a certain direction, and when it stops rolling there is no need to hold it in order to prevent its rolling back. Which is not true if one lifts something. In nature, there are changes of all sorts; man adapts himself to them. Indeed, it does not matter what form the molten silver takes; whether an ingot or a cup, it remains silver. Whereas the splitting of the Red Sea is against nature and has to be constantly sustained for the duration of the crossing, like the Creation of the world itself, which is, of course, the ultimate act against nature.

To change the nature of something, or to perform a miracle, requires the continuous action of a force, and this is true even for things that, in themselves, are not absolute. Thus, for instance, water flows, but ice stands still; nevertheless, I would have to exert some steady force in the realm of temperature, for one, in order for each of them to continue to be what they are.

Thus, too, the Creation of the world is the changing of nothing into something; in order to do so, there must be something, some force, to ensure that the something will not return to its former state of nonbeing. In other words, I have to maintain a constant hold on the nothing, first to change it to its present form and then to make sure it doesn't return to itself.

Creation of the world is not a mere change of form, however; it is an action against the very nature of reality, which is Zero or Nothing. This basic zero state is fundamental; everything that exists is an emergence from the primordial emptiness, and it continues to exist by virtue of the constant force that sustains it. In scientific terms one would say that Creation is the unceasing force opposing entropy.

As has been mentioned, a person has to grow and to keep growing all the time. He stands against the wearing away of the world, its tendency to level out toward zero. In order to exist, one has to create, to be repeatedly born anew, to do something meaningful. Existence itself is thus seen as an unnatural state that has to be maintained; when the force that does so ceases to function, existence ceases. A poetic image of this is in the saying that the world is held in the arms of God. Otherwise, it would fall into the abyss of nothingness.

It might be self-evident that if life is withdrawn the result is death. But even inorganic substance, even dead matter, is dependent on the sustaining force of the Creator. Life, then, can be considered a wondrous thing, but it is only a detail in the miracle of the ongoing existence of the world.

How are we to explain the expression: "You give life to them." The word "You" is directed to that which is so much greater than anything that can be conceived by man; it would be absurd to think we could thereby be expressing the truth of the relation. It would be more correct to say that just as man is greater in his wholeness, than any ten sentences he may utter, so is God more than the Ten Utterances of His act of Creation. The vastness of the unuttered potential is unconceivably greater than that which is expressed, even if it is the Cosmos itself.

Which brings us to the ambivalent relationship of man to faith. On one hand, we feel God to be very near; on the other, as we see, He is very distant. We call Him Father. We also call Him "Ein Sof" (Infinite). Actually, I need both these, especially when I am concerned with the question of Divine Providence. For whenever I move something—even to the slightest degree—it has a reason and a result. As the Tzadik said, lifting up a handful of sand and letting it run out through his fingers: "He who does not believe that every one of these particles returns exactly to the place that God wishes, is a heretic." Another image, attributed to the Baal Shem Tov, says that sometimes a great storm comes, hurls everything about, and causes the trees to shake violently so that the leaves fall. One such leaf may drop close to a worm, and it was for this the whole world was in a furor—that a worm may eat of a certain leaf.

This, then, is the aspect of personal Providence. God's word activates and changes the world all the time; at every moment there is a totally new state of affairs. Whether a microbe or a galaxy, all are equally part of this and are in the same proportion to Him. This means that God is close to us without ceasing; nothing can occur without Him. To be sure, it includes the bad as well as the good. For we need the flow of life in us even when we transgress. So that, on the other hand, there is God the Ein Sof, who gives life to all that is. In both cases we address Him with the same "Thou" or "You"—"You" is both the speaker and the speech, the Ten Utterances and the alphabet, Torah and world.

Clearly, a biblical expression such as "and God said" is not intended to show resemblance between human speech and Divine speech. What is meant is obviously another kind of analogy, and its purpose is to enable us to relate to God and to understand Scripture in a human fashion. Because basically what is being stated is that something has been communicated by God; a certain knowledge or information has been transmitted down from one plane to another.

This particular mode of explanation, rather than a more reverential or poetic one, is deliberately chosen. A metaphor, for instance, is generally used to convey some emotional or poetic relation, and is not to be relied on for precision; that is, every person may interpret it somewhat differently. What we have here is more in the nature of an operative model, something on our own level that will enable us to comprehend what is happening on a higher plane, beyond our comprehension.

As an aside, one may point out that there have been different approaches to this problem, one of them being the rationalist philosophic school. According to this outlook, the scriptural expression is borrowed from human experience only to indicate a certain relation. Expressions such as, "The arm of the Lord," "The breath of Thy nostrils," "His feet stand on the Mount of Olives," etc., state something very general, far too inclusive to be emotionally evocative, and not necessarily human in the sense of an exact description of anything. As Rambam says, rather sagaciously: Phrases like "and God descended," "He came," "and God spoke" are all to be interpreted as modes of revelation.

The Kabbalistic explanation, on the other hand, confirming that the Divine may not be regarded as having a form or body, and in certain ways, even more removed from any concretization than the philosophic approach, sees these scriptural expressions as models. So that in Kabbalistic interpretation there is a meaningful difference between "He stands" and "He dwells" and the like. There are not only emotional ramifications in these distinctions, but also very specific spiritual, intellectual significances. In any event, it is clear that we cannot transfer the image of God speaking to a human level, even though there is an operational resemblance. There has to be a switch over to another plane or dimension of being.

Divine speech appears to the prophet in a manner specific to him. He doesn't necessarily hear precisely these sounds or letters. The communication or prophecy takes the form that the prophet's receptivity is most likely to absorb and comprehend. It may thus be revealed visually as a vision or a figure or a scene, or auditorially as clearly comprehensible speech, or intellectually in terms of symbols, letters, or thought transfer, or even as an idea grasped through the agency of something or someone else. Whatever the medium of transfer, the prophetic message is adapted to the prophet himself.

In all instances it is a force incapable of being described by words or images, even though that is the way it may be

revealed in prophecy. And when it manifests as physical
world, material things are created rather than words: sky or
mountain, man or particle are modes of expressions of Divine
speech in a different medium.

It depends, then, through what instrument the Divine
speech manifests, and on what level it is spoken. Thus, the
combination of letters we read as "Shor" (Ox) may be interpreted in a variety of ways. It may be considered as one of the
four creatures of the Divine Chariot (as in Ezekiel). It can also
be an animal grazing in the field. In a manner of speaking it is
the same ox. The Divine-angelic creature is the same as the
grass-eating beast; it has simply been translated in a different
medium. The ox in each case assumes the features of the
framework in which it is manifesting. In the physical world it
assumes the particularity and limitations of an animal; in the
heavenly world it becomes a holy, angelic, and spiritual entity.

There remains an essential bond between the two, however,
but it is so inward and hidden that only someone who is able
to see things in their deeper reality, like the prophet, can say
that a certain angel has the face of an ox. It is not a matter of
platonic ideas, of an ox-ness as basic essence or as an absolute
in an abstract world. In fact, the combination of letters "shor"
has no more to do with the ox in the field than the angelic being
that emerges from the word "shor." The same thing has been
allowed to emanate in different forms. Let us take an illustration from the realm of geometry. What happens to a simple
form like a circle when it is projected in a variety of different
angles? In one it will preserve the form of a circle; in most it is
likely to lose it and take on entirely different forms. And it is
quite impossible to say that one is better, or more correct, than
another.

What is being stated here is that on all levels of existence, the
Divine speech, whether as words of Torah or as created world,
is always the same thing. The relation between the different
manifestations is very profound; but each is saying the same
thing. God "speaks" in the world, God "speaks" in the Torah.
The difference between them is explained by the fact that what
is known as prophecy comes from another world, the World of
Emanation as it is revealed in the World of Creation. Which

means that the prophet who beholds something and the ordinary man who has a vision of some sort may be seeing the same thing, except that it is not on the same level. The difference depends on two things. The first difference is in the clarity; the prophet sees things in general; the higher and more distinct his vision, the less he sees the interaction in the world with all its complexities. In this sense, the angel is much simpler than man. The angelic creature of the Chariot with the face of an ox is a much simpler being, even though he is much higher than the grass-eating ox in the field, because this latter ox expresses the projections of many worlds, one on top of the other, whereas the angel is himself the thing, that is to say, he is more singular, uncommon, and unencumbered and, therefore, clearer. As it is said, when the Divine speech comes from a higher plane, it is clearer and more comprehensible to the student of Torah.

The second difference is like that which is explained in the introduction to *Tikunei Zohar*. If our world were altogether static, it would express the Divine speech in an even and steady fashion. But since our world is dynamic and—especially as a result of human intervention—rather unstable and disharmonious, the Divine speech is not expressed as it should be. To illustrate, let us imagine an arrangement of letters constituting a text and that this is given over to a band of children. Some of the children move the letters, either by chance or wanton playfulness, so that whatever was written can no longer be deciphered. If fact, the whole concept of Paradise is that of a place or an essence on earth where the proportions or arrangements are undisturbed, perfect and unpolluted by man. It is not a matter of human sin acting as pollution, but rather the misuse of human freedom, of free choice. Because in our freedom to choose, we, who do not know how to read, misplace the letters of Creation and put things in disorder. The task of mitzvot (commandments) of the Torah is to restore order, to arrange things to form a harmony and put every item in its proper place. Chasidism often conveyed this in the form of parable and story, as in the stories of Rabbi Nachman of Bratslav. In short, the world is not functioning properly because things are not where they should be, and the mitzvah is that which enables us to set a specific thing in its own place. Whatever you do, perform it according to a certain order or design. Because these patterns, as indicated in the Torah, are intended to restore the order of the world. The Torah thus serves as a map that represents, not an existing reality, but an ideal one. The ideal reality is that which the world aspires to become. And the forms of this perfected world are those that permit the utmost freedom of action and on which the Torah can have the greatest effect.

Everything thus has a soul, and the soul of a thing is the Divine speech that speaks the thing, either directly or as an echo or as a re-echoing refrain. The Divine speech says: the sun, the stone, the tree—and if one studies it carefully one can comprehend the relation between the revealed form of sun, stone, or tree, and that inward thing that is its animating soul.

On one hand, then, everything is an expression of the Divine. There is nothing, but His speech. On the other hand, the table *is* a table, the chair *is* a chair, I *am* I. And this latter common-sense seeing is very much a matter of the seer and the angle of vision; even if it doesn't say anything certain about the object, it truthfully reflects the subject and the modes of perception.

Moreover, the reality of the world is nowadays apprehended in terms of electromagnetic fields. But when I look at the world I do not see electromagnetic fields, nor do I perceive any diagrammatic representation of a mathematical formula; what I see is, again, table, chair, arm, and leg. Which is to say that my organs of perception do not see. And it is known that our vision is limited to a narrow range of light-waves of a certain size. From which we may conclude that we have to use our understanding to see that which our vision cannot ascertain.

In the same way, since the eyes of the body cannot hope ever to see the Holy One, Blessed be He, the problem is one of using the right means of explanation. All too often the wrong tools are used to describe or illumine certain concepts, as for instance, to say that an intelligence is so complex that it cannot be touched. It becomes absurd because intelligence is not touchable. The two essences do not belong together.

The fact that we perceive things as tangible solids is a reflection of our own incapacity to see their spiritual essence, which has quite another appearance. There are two levels of perception. One is the grasp of the actuality of matter as solids in which certain forces are at work. The other is the recognition that solid matter is an illusion of the senses, and that reality consists of a relation between certain forces or energies. What is more, the force that animates the thing is the thing; without it, the thing would not be. It is not only a matter of a relation between matter and spirit, but rather that matter, or the world, is itself Divine speech.

From this point of view, there is nothing else but God; only He exists, and the world we know is an aspect of His speech as perceived by our senses. Which does not mean that the world does not exist as world or that it is an illusion. On the contrary, the world is very real indeed; it is objective and true, even if not necessarily material and self-sustaining. The paradox, as seen by the mind, can be reduced to the questions put by both the philosophers and the Kabbalists concerning the relation between the world and God. If we presume one, how can the other exist? It is an insoluble problem for both. If the world is God speaking to Himself, then God remains alone even after Creation, and matter is only another form of eternal spirit and there is no contradiction between them. Indeed, both matter and spirit are external manifestations—to say that God is spiritual is just as erroneous as to say that God is material, for no quality may pertain to Him as the ultimate reality. Both matter and spirit are modes of Divine projection, emanations of certain aspects of His being. He Himself, as said, cannot be described or defined in any way.

Divine speech is therefore the only objective reality. The forms we recognize as real are dependent on our instruments of perception. If we had other instruments of perception, we would surely apprehend another world entirely. Just as an angel probably sees a different world, or a donkey, or even different kinds of men. That which is perceived may thus be considered of secondary importance; what is significant is that there does exist a world that is the object of our perception and that is somehow "real." The problem, then, remains—what is the relation between this grasped reality and the Divine speech that is beyond grasp, but in whose existence we must believe?

To illustrate the nature of a possible answer, let us consider the sun and its light. This light of the sun illumines the earth, and it also gives the sun itself its radiance; one can hardly say that the light of the earth illumines the sun. In this sense, the light we receive, even though its source is in the sun itself, does not add anything or detract. Its use is totally given over to cause and effect; if the light is blocked, there is no illumination. The light itself does not have to do any illuminating; it gives light to things because it is itself light. The point being made here is that the amount of light revealed on earth exists to the same extent in the sun; it is just that in the sun it is insignificant, swallowed up in the vastly greater light of its origin, while on earth, because there is distance—and this is all we have of the source of all life—we relate to it accordingly. Which then serves as an illustration for the life that comes from God. In spite of the fact that He is the Creator of all that is, it is all as nothing to God, reduced as it is to insignificance by His infinity. In other words, the truth of the matter is that the Divine did not create something out of nothing. He created "nothing" out of something that is Himself.

The nothingness of the world is not necessarily an objective evaluation. From the perspective of man, it is nothing because it is beyond his grasp; from the perspective of God, it is nothing because it is so insignificant. Objectively, there does seem to be some sort of gradation, from greater light to lesser light down to the various facets of the world. Very often, however, we see objects, or wretchedness, rather than light. We fail to see that that which exists as objectively real for us is another expression of the Divine, of His holiness and His will. Indeed, in order for man to accept the world as real—rather than nothing—it has to be seen as having meaning, that is, sanctity.

The world may thus be considered as "something" because the true nothing is somewhere at a zero point in between man and God. We are a certain "something" who is aware of both what He is and what we are.

3

The Nullification of Reality

To better grasp the idea of any existence in the light of God, we return to the paradox. The light of the sun illuminates everything everywhere; does it not also do so on the sun itself? And the answer, of course, is that it does not even have any existence on the sun, much less an effect. The globe of the sun is the source — it cannot be anything else — whereas the light of the sun coming out of it has distinctiveness only at some distance away. When the ray of sunlight is still close to, or lodged in, the sun-globe, it is undistinguishable as something separate; it doesn't exist as yet. Only as it separates and recedes from the sun, only when it has its own space, does it begin to exist of itself.

All of which is to illustrate the relation between that reality that is existent, and the nothing, the nonexistent. Just as light takes on existence only when it is separated from its source, so is the reality of the world meaningful only as it is cut off from its source in the Divine. The world is something distinct and real because of the gap between, because it is not lodged any longer within God but has been emanated from God.

The light of the sun exists only because of its separation from the sun. The nearer to the sun anything gets, the less does it possess an independent reality. In human terms, one could say, "No man shall look upon Me and live." No one can approach God beyond a certain distance. And it is not a matter of physical capacity; the impossibilty is a function of the very essence of things. One cannot remain a human being and see the face of the Divine. For as soon as I approach God, I cease to be something separate. Neither terror nor fearfulness is involved. It is simply not possible to be in two places at the same time. Our being human depends on this distance from God. To give another example: in any play of light and shadow, the distinctiveness of form depends on maintaining a minimal distance from the source of light; as soon as one gets too close, the whole thing is dissolved and made unfeasible. The sin of the sons of Aaron—who approached the Ark of the Covenant and died—was that they crossed a certain border, beyond which one may not venture and live. This is connected incidentally, with a basic idea of Judaism, that one has to be careful not to cross this boundary between man and God, because if one does, one cannot return.

Can it be concluded, then, that the Holy One, Blessed be He, has to exert His powers in order to support the existence of each and every thing in the world, and that there is no such thing as freedom? To which it may be answered that it all depends on what one means by freedom, or independence. In the confines of Providence, the independence of the world is considerably restricted. And whatever limited sort of independence there is, it exists for man only in the matter of the freedom to choose between good and evil. Which, in itself, demands that people be of a certain caliber, able to make such a decision.

As for the freedom from the laws of nature, it is again to be understood in relation to the reality of a continous Creation—and the definition of miracle. Because, in fact, there is no such thing as miracle in the sense of either defying or repudiating natural law. Natural law is merely the persistence of Creation within a relatively fixed framework. A somewhat inadequate metaphor would be to say that if the world is Divine speech, then the laws of nature are like the rules of grammar. These rules determine the framework—they are not binding laws that cannot be defied. They serve a purpose, and for the most part speech follows their directives, even if occasionally there are digressions. There may even be transgressions. One of the books dealing with the problem from a mystical point of view claims that fresh interpretations of the Torah are the roots of miracle and that the repetition of Torah is like the repetition of nature's laws. Consequently, a new interpretation is like what we would call a mutation. Just as in all mutations, it continues to function according to law. The point to be emphasized is that nature and the laws of nature are fixed within a certain repetitive cycle, a statistical determinism that remains more or less the same in spite of the fact that each part or particle can decide for itself to make or not to make a certain limited move within its orbit.

In a certain sense, free choice is largely dependent on the sustained reliability of Nature. Were the world fluctuating and unstable, and Divine Will revealed in an arbitrary fashion, then free choice would be practically impossible. He who transgresses knows that he thereby cuts himself off from his source of life and that sin is death, in simple terms. But he can do it! The very possibility of free choice is largely dependent on the fixedness of the world, on the fact that one can rely on it. There is a description in some book of the Sages, of the lecher, who not only commits a sin, but in doing so compels God to create another one like himself. Nature is thus an accomplice, a necessary part of the system of free choice. If someone wanted to deprive men of their freedom to choose, it could be accomplished, not by denying them the possibility to choose, but by questioning the authenticity of their resolve. Because free choice takes place in a world in which the omniscient God is not visible and His actions are not manifest.

Notwithstanding, it is said that the Torah was forced on Israel like a mountain tumbled on their heads. And the fact is that God's will, the tumbling of a mountain on man, does not leave much room for human choice. This does not mean that free choice is denied; it is rather that the human possibility to choose is dependent again on the availability of certain things. When one sees God, for example, what else can one do but acquiesce? True, they did accept His dominion, but it was done willingly and it wasn't forced on them, even if it came tumbling about their heads like a mountain. This, incidentally, is the meaning of the saying that at the end of days the freedom of choice will no longer be necessary or desirable. Similarly, too, it is said that although the worship of God may be greater in the time of the Messiah, the worship of God in our time is more precious, the difference being that nature and the laws of nature make it possible to choose. The miracle only serves to upset the balance of things so that if there is too much of it, an excess of Divine action, then free choice departs completely.

Moreover, in order to make a drastic change in the laws of nature, to make a miracle, an entirely new world has to be created. The Talmud has an account of such a dilemma—in the story of Rabbi Elazar, who was very poor and complained to God about it. And God told him that if he wished things to be different, the whole world would have to be destroyed and rebuilt in order for Rabbi Elazar's luck to take a turn for the better. To which Rabbi Elazar replied that he preferred to renounce his personal needs and to let the world remain as it was.

It might be in place here to return to the problem of being and nonbeing. On the one hand, it is not said that the world does not exist, but rather that the being of the world does not have existence. To grasp the distinction, it is necessary to comprehend a basic concept of Chabad Chasidism, that of the "nullification of existence." This does not mean a repudiation of one's reality, which, even on a much higher level, is unacceptable. The nullification of reality or of existence relates to the way one sees oneself, to the repudiation of oneself as an independent entity not dependent on God. In fact, the whole problem of being and nonbeing should not be viewed in terms of existence or reality; there is no leveling out or repudiation of that which is, but rather a repudiation of the being or nonbeing of desire. The world, in other words, is not "Maya" or an illusion in the Oriental sense. It is simply that what one sees as world is a product of incorrect seeing; were one able to perceive it differently, not through the physical senses, an entirely different world would be grasped, a world on a higher level, as Divine speech. Because the relations between things in the world are the relations between the letters of the Divine utterance in all their derivative forms and images. It is in this sense that the world can be considered as nothing and of no substance.

What, then, is "nothing and of no substance"? Actually, it is a material image that the mind of man considers as fundamental. We start with the basis that things are or are not. And even if something is in the category of not being, it is seen as an accretion to the fundamental reality of material being. Because perception is of the eyes of the flesh and sees material objects.

Theoretically, this is not absolutely necessary; we could have more subtle means of perception—as indeed there are, even among living men, those who see a vastly richer, more expanded world, whether material or spiritual. Indeed, even ordinary persons perceive much more of the spiritual than is believed. It is just that the reality doesn't get adequate response from our consciousness. The fact is that we never see a unified monolithic world of matter. For we are located at the extreme limits of the domain in which the Divine is hidden, there where it is still possible to extricate oneself. If we had no status beyond that of matter, it would be beyond our capacities to get out of it. Even in our present position, we scarcely have enough words and intellectual equipment to move a little out of the framework of unmitigated physicality. For instance, were our senses really sensitive, let us say, to energy waves of a broader spectrum, our world would undoubtedly be entirely different and far less rigid. In a manner of speaking, this position of ours is a part of something that builds an entire concept of reality; it is Pharaoh, King of Egypt saying, "The Nile is mine and I made myself." This view of existent reality—that I made myself and that the world belongs to me—seems to be a concept of the utmost arrogance of being. A person on another level of existence accepts that someone else made him. "Making oneself" intimates that all of reality, all the world, is a product of one's own will and it has its own laws, without relation to other worlds. This distorted picture of reality is prevalent enough, a product of our "eyes of flesh," our physically restricted perception, and the fact of our being so far from the light of the source. But as soon as we approach the light, it loses all meaning and evaporates.

We think of the concrete and the material as though it were something absolute, because our grasp of being and nonbeing is that it is identical with reality and the absence of reality. Whereas, being is actually that which has independence, whose existence does not depend on something else. And nonbeing, or nothing, is that which is the very opposite. The fact that one sees matter as the primary aspect of the real makes for a world that is actually at a distance from reality and that is inappropriately called Being.

Therefore, when we speak of the nullification of Being, it does not mean taking that which is and smashing it. It signifies rather that the less the I assumes priority in the conscious mind, the more there is a nullification of Being.

In response to a question concerning the idea of "Unio-Mystica"—the total obliteration of oneself—it may be said that it is not given to us to accomplish it in this world. And in Judaism, whatever can be known of such "Union" exists only in one condition—within the mitzvah. True, there are those who think that only a person who reaches a degree of unio-mystica can truly fulfill the mitzvot.

The explanation is that the mitzvah is itself Divine unity. And the illustration is given of someone who is clasped by the king, held in his embrace for a moment—in which case it doesn't matter what clothes He is wearing; it is the arm of the king that counts. Just as, when I busy myself with Torah, it doesn't matter what the physical trappings of the book are. The essential thing is the word of God that comes through. And as soon as Torah enters my mind, I become united with it.

Thus, too, what is the difference between greatness and smallness in a person? It is a matter of the degree of consciousness of that which is happening at the moment. When a person performs a mitzvah, he is united in some way or other with God. Which seriously raises another question: To what extent can a person overleap the gap between man and God? For if a human being does make this leap, he is no longer human. The answer to this question is that such a "unity" can exist for man, only in terms of a higher aspect of his humanity. It is as though after death, a man were to be confronted with an alternative:

whether he wants or doesn't want Paradise. Those ordinary small persons who want Paradise for themselves are those who wish to have the Divine, certainly, but at a safe distance. Only the great ones among men are ready to renounce Paradise in their wish to be absorbed and extinguished in God.

Now the self-extinguishing in God is a nullification of even the highest self, and this, it would seem, is the highest level of renunciation. And since, as it is indicated, the great unity comes from Torah and mitzvot, this would seem to have priority. In other words, it depends on man himself. He who lays tefillin, for example, binds himself thereby to God, and it doesn't matter what he comprehends of the mitzvah of tefillin. The question, as stated by another sage, of whether the tefillin is in the head or on the head belongs to another category—the two levels of being are mutually exclusive. Just as in accepting that the world is entirely pervaded by the Divine, one may conclude that nothing more is needed.

Another interesting Kabbalistic idea is related to the oddly recurrent notion that the tefillin are connected with the mystery of the biblical story of the cuttings, made by Jacob, on the rods that he placed before the flocks at the watering trough, making the animals bear striped and spotted offspring. No one else can ever do such a thing with a stick. But, theoretically, it means that Divine unity can be accomplished through any object or thing in the world. It simply places a human being in a situation of the supreme challenge to his humanity, one that he cannot cope with, and so he has to return to the way of Torah and mitzvot. Behind which is the question concerning the extent to which a man can reach Divine union without spilling over into illusory union. Because a person can attain a very high level of subjective delight without this having any effect on his relation to the Divine. In a way, it can even be presumed that where there is great pleasure, one doesn't see much else besides oneself.

In answer to the question about the "nullification of reality," what is implied is actually a renouncing of one's will, or a repudiation of one's own will making His will ours. It means that in wanting something (for one's self), one coerces the higher will to it and shatters the sense of one's real self. Whereas in nullifying the primacy of that which is desired, one is admitting that something else is more important, more valuable. Which in turn transforms the act of renunciation into an act of free will and inner expression.

4

Concealment as Part of Creation

To grasp the metaphoric image of God as both sun and shield, it is necessary to see God as so bright that everything would be burnt up in Him were it not for the protection of an "atmosphere." At the end of days, when the shield or sheath will be removed, the wicked will be punished and the righteous will be restored. For the combination of sun and shield serve to bring light and heat in sufficient quantity so as to avoid injury to life. Both the revelation and the concealment, or shield, are necessary to assert the existence of God to man. The first is the sacred Name itself (translated as Lord) and the second is *Elokim* (God), which protects the world from the power of the Name.

"The meaning of the name (YHVH) is 'that which brings everything into existence ex nihilo.' " The letter *yod* before the root *Havaya* (to be) indicates constancy of action, continuous being rather than single action. An example of such usage is to be found in the Book of Job (1:5), where the *yod* does not show future tense, as it ordinarily does, but a continuity of doing "all the days."

Creation is thus not to be understood as a single action performed in the Six Days of Genesis. It is a continuous process; God keeps creating the world all the time. And this is the very meaning of His Name, the sacred name that is considered the creative power behind all that is.

Among the descriptive names of God we may here mention "The Great" and "The Mighty." The attribute of Chesed (Grace or Love) in the system of the ten Sefirot is also known as Greatness. In other words, Chesed is not only "loving-kindness" in the sense of goodness of heart; it is essentially the power of giving, the source of plenty and of all bounty in terms of substance and influence. All giving as positive action is Chesed. It is not restricted to charity or goodness, although it includes them, of course. It embraces the power and spiritual capacity to offer to, or confer upon, to dispense and pour out. Therefore, too, it is the creative force, while Gevurah (Strength), the following and opposite Sefirah, is also known as Awe (of God), Fear, or Judgment. It is the attribute of control, of preventing excess; by fixing proper boundaries and restraints into life, the forces of life are contained and made potent. Where Chesed is almost totally outgoing, Gevurah tends to be interiorizing. Necessarily, then, these two Sefirot have extensive emotional overtones and are known also as Love and Awe, respectively. Love is the generous outpouring of feeling from the self to outer reality, while Awe or Fear is a withholding or restriction of feeling, a kind of spasm of contraction.

Concerning the question of effort in relation to cultivating Chesed and Gevurah, it should be evident that it is not that which is in any way decisive. What is important is concentration. The Sefirah of Gevurah is called Strength only by virtue of the power and the greatness of the previous Sefirah of Chesed, which has to be confined and channeled within definite borders in order for it to have any effect. The strength of Gevurah is essentially a function of pointedness, of force withheld, directed, and focussed at will. As it is said: Who is the hero— he who controls his impulses. The dam halting the flow and compelling it to move in a desired direction is the essence of the power that is Gevurah.

In any case, these two Sefirot—Chesed and Gevurah—are basic forces in life, one flowing out of the self and the other withdrawing into the self, controlling and restraining. Each can be used either for good or bad. For example, one of the distortions of Chesed is the sin of fornication, while the Sefirah of Gevurah or Fear (of God) can also be expressed in a variety of questionable ways. Thus, the Tzadik of Lublin once said that when a person falls from the level of Chesed he becomes a lecher; when a person falls from the level of Gevurah, he becomes a murderer. There is also the matter of basic temperament, of course, something a person does not easily change; one can, at best, alter the expression, for good or bad, of temperament or character. Thus, the same person who is constitutionally of a Chesed type may grow in goodness to become a "Chesed Avraham" character, or he may become a profligate "Don Juan" personality. As certain midrashic interpretations have put it: There are both Abraham and Ishmael—Chesed as liberal kindness of heart and Chesed as lustful indulgence. Following Chesed is the Sefirah of Gevurah (Isaac), showing restraint and withdrawal into oneself; its opposite, or the sin of Esau, is murder. There is an inner connection between the extremes, a world full of different modes of expression. In praying to God as *HaGadol ve'HaGibor*, the Great and the Mighty, we are addressing these two Sefirot as they are portrayed by the two Patriarchs—that of graciousness, of complete giving, and that of restraint and control.

This same attribute of Chesed, of giving, is also the basis of Creation; by it the world is continually being made anew and sustained. According to the esoteric wisdom, Chesed springs from the very essence of Godhead; it animates the world in all its details, down to the minutest parts. The cosmos may thus be seen as a manifestation of His unlimited abundance and goodness, the goodness being a constant, not only because He is good but also because He does good. Unlike the general kindliness toward the world, which one may feel without any obligation to do anything about it, the attribute of Chesed is a love that has to express itself in concrete action and specific circumstances. It is in such manner, too, that God nourishes the world—by Chesed Chinam, a free and unqualified giving without regard as to whether it is deserved or how it is used, an infinite kindness, which is Greatness.

All of which is essentially beyond our capacity to under-
stand. Firstly, because we, as mortals, cannot imitate the act of
Creation. Secondly, because the concept of something formed
out of nothing is beyond our grasp, and we are only saying
words without ever being able to experience their meaning.
The meaning, as hinted, being that it is the expression of
Gedulah (Greatness), which is the other name for infinite
Chesed and Goodness.

In other words, it is not a matter of some fabulous trick or
sleight of hand; it is the very inwardness of God emanating
into finite forms. Just as one cannot grasp the essence of God's
infinite reality, so is it impossible to grasp the truth of any of
His attributes. For with man, attributes are qualities that may
be separated from the person and may come and go in the life
of a person. In God, the attributes are intrinsic; they are a part
of His unity and cannot be separated from Him. Thus, even
though Chesed is not identical with God, still, when God
manifests in Chesed, it is in total unity with Him.

To be sure, this may become a matter of some controversy in
regard to certain forms of religious poetry (for example,
Selichot, Neilah), where God's attributes are addressed as something separate. Nevertheless, this basic unity of God and His
attributes remains, for us, the way God reveals Himself. The
attribute of Chesed, for instance, is not any particular behavior
pattern or emotion by itself; it is a Divine manifestation
through Grace, Love, Kindness.

No created intellect, whether of man or angel, can possibly
bridge the gap between the works of Creation and the Creator.
Just as the creature is unable to grasp the Infinite Divine, so is
it unable to grasp His attributes. Indeed, when speaking of any
of the Divine attributes or Sefirot, we are only bringing the
incomprehensible down to our human level because we are
confronted with an insoluble dilemma. We can either use terms
that are obviously imprecise and incorrect, but have some
meaning for us as humans, or we can try to use precise terms
that only make us totally inarticulate, unable even to begin to
express ourselves. In a sense, as soon as one wishes to be
absolutely correct in speech, there are no words any longer,
none that satisfy the requirements.

To illustrate the concept of a lack of words, let us take a fact from the world of physics. Light waves have different lengths, and the ultraviolet light waves, for instance, are known to be invisible to us. There are certain creatures, such as bees, however, who can see at least some of these ultraviolet light waves. In short, part of that which, for us, is total darkness is for them light. Now the question is: What kind of light or darkness is it? We are in a situation where we have no words, or even concepts, to describe something, a color, that obviously exists.

In like manner, we can say that there are no words to describe the Transcendent. But since, as we believe, God does wish to have some contact with us, He is prepared to suffer the imprecision of our language. There is the little story—within another context perhaps, but aptly descriptive—of one of the Tzadikim who suddenly stopped his prayers at a point where there was no pause. When asked why he did so, he answered with a parable. Once a king passed and saw a beggar playing a fiddle, and the tune pleased him so much that he stopped and invited the beggar to the palace to play before him. Now this beggar had an old fiddle with strings that broke easily, so that people told him that it was not respectful to the king to play on it before him, and it would be better to make alterations and at least fix the strings. At which the beggar answered: "If the king wants a tune on a fine instrument, he does not lack better musicians than I; if he asked me to play before him, he took into consideration the poor state of my fiddle as well as my own limitations." Thus, too—if, as we surmise, God wishes to hear our prayers, and our sincere speech with Him—He suffers our anthropomorphisms, that is, our calling on Him by names that are human and in terms that are limited in their expressiveness. We say: If you want us, take us as we are with all our faults and inadequacies; it is the best we have to offer. The only thing we can do beyond that is to know that certain things are not exact or true, and to be grateful for the privilege (and the audacity) to say them.

Thus, something in our human speech can approach the reality and greatness of the Divine. When speaking of God's Chesed or any other quality, one does not get any closer to understanding. As Rambam says, there is only an identity of words, which can be more of a misguidance than truth. For just as we give names to the stars in the heavens, so is there no comparison between our names for the attributes of God—Chochmah (Wisdom), Chesed (Grace), etc.—and the reality they depict; it is simply as close as we can get. It is much less than a model or even an analogy. I have some idea of what Chesed means for me, and esoteric knowledge claims that there exists some sort of relation between this and the Divine attribute, but in actuality there is a vast distance between them, which I cannot pretend to have traversed.

To be sure, it may be claimed that I am a product of Divine grace. If so, how is it that I do not have a way of knowing Him? It is as though a creature of three dimensions were to draw a picture of two dimensions. This two-dimensional picture could never grasp the concept of three dimensions or comprehend that which brought it into existence. We, too, are thus a sort of transfer or a projection from some higher plane of being, constantly receiving from it and even endeavoring to grow into it, but altogether unable ever to grasp it or understand it.

However, if I receive from it, there is some relation between us. True, but the philosophic questions involved are endless: What is creation of the finite from the infinite? How can things retain their separate form? Why do we not become utterly absorbed in the Oneness of the Unity? And can something exact and specific emerge from something that belongs to another order of existence? How can the known produce the unknown?

In other words, it may be said that from the relation between the power of creation, which has no limit, and the power of withdrawal, which is also unlimited, there is formed the limited. The limited is formed from the relation between the plus and the minus of infinity, which meet somehow between being and nonbeing, between the existence that is absolute and a nothing that is also absolute, as a segment cutting through and creating all these manifold existences that are actually neither total something nor total nothing and are called creations.

The meaning of which is that just as we cannot understand

the infinity of the manifest, we cannot understand the infinity of the unmanifest, the hidden. Just as we cannot understand the meaning of the name of God as "I Am," we cannot understand the name of God as the shield and the shielded, the crystallized world of actuality and the mystery surrounding everything. As it is written, concerning the concept of God as the hidden one, He is also the One who oscillates between light and darkness, who is infinite and who creates a finite world out of the interaction between His two aspects of Being.

Every existence becomes known to us as such only when its Divine aspect is diminished; there has to be a limit where one gives way to the other. If, then, there is no direct communication with God, no possible understanding of the Divine without a way of expressing the God within, what kind of connection do we have? To which it may be answered that since our component parts are divine, we are a part of God. And being a part of Him, we can devise some sort of communication with God. It is just that this communication does not penetrate the realm of our minds in the sense that it can formulate things as whole entities. What, then, do we live by? We live by those shadows, or figments, that we can grasp, that we can make contact with, little as it is. Because that which we grasp is a positive essence. Clinging to it, we do not declare the world to be a lie, a delusion; we simply accept that though sometimes it is dark and evil, it is still Divine manifestation. We are bound to both aspects of the world, that which is and that which is not, the manifest and the unmanifest, for they are intrinsically one. Our specific existence simply depends on our being somewhere in between—we draw sustenance from it, we never entirely belong to either realm, we never arrive at our journey's end. On the other hand, that which we contain within our grasp is true—it is not a falsehood; it is only a product of our being where we are, and we cannot overleap it. We are an expression of the Divine and yet it is not given to us to comprehend it.

We stand on the other side of an abyss, formed by the very act of Creation. As it is said, "And no man shall see Me and live." So that as soon as I cross the abyss, I cease to be a human being. And it is not necessarily a matter of man seeing beings of the angelic order, but rather of growth. For what is the highest revelation possible to a man? It is the revelation of his own soul. And when a man reaches such a supreme revelation of his soul, he ceases to be a man. Which is again the same paradox. A person lives by virtue of his soul, but he can never really approach it. So that we are forever enjoying only the sparks of the great fire and remain fearful to come too close to it. And if we ever do come too close, we cease to exist. In this sense, we are always holding on to something, except that this something is so distant, so disconnected, that our expressions are always partial and inadequate. The other side of the matter is that if we were not created thus, we could never attain, to such a degree of speech, a capacity of even conceiving such thoughts. The fact that we can even relate to the very essence of faith stems from the fact that we are a part of the Divine. Our very speech flows from this vital source, but here are also the limitations. Were we, God forbid, creatures of the Devil (not that we believe there are such creatures, or that there is a Devil—in spite of a lot of credible evidence to the contrary), we would not be able to speak about that which we are conversing. The little we are able to talk about God is by virtue of the fact that a part of us is of God, even though the rest of us is a creature of God. Between these two, in this extremely narrow gap, are we bidden to overcome the barrier of our humanity. Every such overcoming, every Divine relation in us, every indication of that which we relate to as holy, is the success of the Divine.

Elsewhere in the *Tanya* it is written that what God demands of us is to reach our own "beyond," our own infinite dimension, and not to reach His infinity. The writer urges us to get out from the confines of the created and to go beyond—the passage being that which binds us to God. The mitzvah is one such passageway or connecting link, like a hand outstretched by the Divine. While any of the expressions of martyrdom is another way we have to connect with Him. In both of these, we find the infinite that lies within the finite; something of Divine essence is made available to us. Which is the other side of the statement "And ye shall be as gods." For if man were totally cut off from God, there would be no meaning to Divine revelations or even to His Creation. The meaning of the Creation of man and of man's worship of God—of Divine revelation altogether—rests on the fact that in spite of all the hiddenness of God, we do have a way of reaching the infinite. And it is even possible, in certain instances, to reach Him precisely within the hiddenness.

The paradox here being considered is that the true unlimited and infinite and incomprehensible is not Divine creation, but the Divine hiddenness. A greater mystery than reality is the concealment of reality. As has been said: The glory of God is perhaps the fact that among the rest of Creation there can also be an unbeliever, who denies God even though he lives by the mercy of God and reveals God with every breath of his nostrils or twitch of his finger. That such a creature should have the capacity to deny the existence of God is an expression of God's infinite power.

In which respect there is a talmudic discussion around certain different modes of addressing God in the Bible. Moses said: The Great, the Almighty, and the Terrible. Certain prophets, noting that awful things were done on earth by man, asked: Where is His Greatness, where is His Might? So that in Jeremiah, for instance, there is no mention of Greatness. In Daniel, there is no mention of Might. And the sages of the Great Assembly in a later generation restored His Glory when they declared: That is His Might that He can hear the insult against him and be silent. This then is the other meaning of Might—as the Darkness, the indifference to light. If someone can see the infinite in the darkness and not in the light—that is a manifestation of Divine might or power.

In another manner of speaking, this is also an explanation, not of the way of the soul, but of the way of Divine reality. Why should man find God in the time of a crisis, out of the darkness in his life? Because there is a kind of finding that acts in the dark and not in the light. There are situations when there is an abundance of positive things and one would think that it would be easier to see the Divine. But it seems that God is further away at such times than in periods of stress and strain, when darkness dispels all goodness and joy.

Although to be sure, there aren't two separate states—one in which God is manifest and another, of opposite character, in which He is absent. It is rather that since He "creates light and forms the darkness" equally, and the miracle of darkness is like unto the miracle of light, and just as we don't understand the wonder of light, of that which is, we do not comprehend the wonder of that which is not, of the nothing. We cannot understand the mystery of the withdrawal of the Divine that is the essence of Power.

How can we call Him "Great" if some person who is created can rise up and deny the Creator? And how can we call him the Almighty if there is a world that seems to keep going of itself. When Kabbalists say that, in *gematria* (reckoning the numerical value of the letters of a word) God is Nature, they add as though in jest, that Nature (Teva) is that in which the manifestation of God gets drowned (Tovei'ah). In this sense, God is the order, the unity, the regulating factor. All of which is part of the hiddenness of God; the order of the world is a part of His concealment. The power to see the infinite, that which is beyond limit and beyond order in the limits and regularity of the world, is a manifestation of the Great and the Almighty.

Which explains how it is possible that, on one hand, all our being is nothing but Divine, while all our existence is unable to reach anything approaching the Divine.

Just as we do not grasp the power of Creation or the nature of Divine influence altogether, which is infinite benevolence, so are we incapable of grasping His hiddenness and withdrawal, which is called Tzimtzum. This latter attribute of Gevurah (Might), as we have said, is the opposite of Gedulah (Greatness, Loving-kindness)—for Gedulah or Chesed is directed outward from within, while Gevurah, which is also Pachad (Fear) or Yirah (Awe), is the withdrawal inward. The difference between them is the difference between expansion and contraction. What, then, is the power of Gevurah if it is a movement of contraction and self-withdrawal and reluctance to reveal? It is the power of giving life and existence in the knowledge that the creature comes from the Creator—even if this is hidden. The attribute of contraction thus extends the essence of Divine revelation by paradoxically concealing its power.

The Divine essence is not openly manifest in vital, life-giving power; it is hidden within it. At the same time, the impression is created that the reality of the world, on all its levels, whether physical or spiritual, is made of some substance. We simply do not see that which is hidden in this world of ours, that everything in the world or beyond is an appearance, a manifestation of Divine light. We regard all things as objects having an existence of their own. They come and go, do whatever they have to do, and, in any event, impress us with the fact of their being solid and real. In short, our sense of reality is derived from things and not from the Divine light. For this light is not at all apparent in things. What we see is a result of the fact that the Divine light constantly changes, divesting itself of form and clothing itself with the form of something else, not necessarily spiritual. One aspect of all this is precisely this transition from the spiritual to the material, from the unlimited to the limited. And this is only a partial division. Both in regard to the spiritual and the natural, our primary point of departure is that all these things are independent entities, that is to say, it is not only that the table is a table, but that it is clear to me that the table exists in and of itself and does not require any other reality to make it so. On the contrary, any analysis and thought on my part has to begin with the world, with the reality I perceive as concrete, and from there I proceed to other things, attainable and unattainable.

So that our understanding of the world is based on the fact that it exists, that things are there of themselves and their existence is a given condition. I can consider and discuss matters of causality and transcendence as much as I like; it will never sound convincing because, ultimately, the more I proceed to mentalize, the further I depart from the realm of the concrete, the real, and find myself in the realm of the abstract. But since things do not really exist except as they are illumined by Divine light, the wonder is that this light is so well hidden that not only do I not have any conception of its existence, but that its existence does not seem to have any meaning at all. I

see things, objects, a world, and I fail to perceive anything of
God in all this, so that when someone claims to have seen a
miracle, some manifestation of God in the world, his seeing is
questioned, not the meaning of what he saw. If someone
nevertheless believes, the question is rather: How can one not
see the Divine manifestation? How is it possible for the world
to exist by itself, of itself? As it has been said: This is the result
of the fact that the Divine light contracts to such an extent. And
the essential factor in this contraction is not that of size or
quantity or even of form, but in the matter of manifestation.
The contraction is, in a way, that which occurs when the
essence of the doer is no longer visible. One could even say that
the problem of the Holy One, Blessed be He, in the world, is to
appear always incognito. His problem is to remain unrecog-
nized. So that when He does appear in the world, it should be
without anyone knowing that it is He. How can He do this?
How can it be that we do not feel the emanation of His essence
and spirituality?

I do not feel that any of the things in the world are the works
of God, His constant creations. I have the feeling that they are
things in themselves. However, this is the real power of God to
whom all is possible – to so contract and conceal His light that
the created thing will not be nullified out of existence, that it
will remain itself, its own thing as far as we are concerned. In
fact, the very condition for the existence of all the multifarious
creatures and objects in the universe, on all the planes of
cosmic being, is that each thing should feel independent.
Without going into the matter of free will, which is an additional condition granted to certain creatures, we shall restrict
ourselves to created things that feel themselves to exist as such,
because they sense they are not God. The very essence of
creatureliness is the feeling of being separate, of being itself.
And this capacity of a thing to be itself, even though its very life
and existence, physically and spiritually, are incessantly dependent on Divine mercy, on His Chesed, is the miracle of His
concealment, His apparent withdrawal. It is as though a
person's arm were to begin to talk back to him and say, "I want
this. I do not want that." Our various organs are a part of the
world, they belong to the things in the world, yet they cannot

be said to have a feeling of independence, nor do they feel that they are something in themselves.

In this respect there are several levels of being, as we know. There is the level on which a certain authority or permission (to act in His name) is granted by God, for instance—as in the world of Briah (Creation), the World of the Throne or of Angels. When the Angel or the Seraf—even though he too is a created thing—realizes that he is an independent creature, he also recognizes the existence of God and is aware of the way the Divine Will functions. Thus, the sense of self is not nullified. Even when he cries out "Holy, Holy, Holy," it is done out of his own volition and power, his own genuine desire to serve. The angel retains a self, even while recognizing the Divine omnipotence and plenty. On the lower levels of being (Formation, Action), the feeling of Divine essence is much weaker and the sense of self is much more pronounced—even to such an extent, as in our human world, that one is able to feel only oneself and be unaware of God altogether. And this latter condition is the extreme of what is known as Tzimtzum, the Divine contraction or withdrawal.

The point being made here is that both of these facts are true, that the created object, the creature, is being created every moment from nothing, and that it isn't even aware of being created. On the contrary, it views itself as being a thing in itself, oblivious to the existence of the forces acting on it.

The problem stems from the fact that there are creatures without consciousness, without awareness of self or even intelligence—in the sense that the lack of intelligence deprives one of the chance to know anything about oneself or about Divine unity. On the other hand, one can say that a creature of small intelligence knows more about the Divine life-force than a man can know. There is a midrashic exegesis to the effect that once David the King walked by the river and congratulated himself on being so full of praises of God. A frog came forth and said: But I praise God more than you! In connection with which a certain sage, Rabbi Zadok Hacohen, remarked: It is not that the frog says prayers to God more than David the King, but that, since the frog has no evil impulse, but does the will of God, and only the Divine Will, in everything, its very existence is a song of praise to God and every croak expresses it. So that a frog can say to a man, even if it be David the Singer of Psalms, that it praises God more than he does. Because no matter how eloquent and inspired a person is, there are moments in life when a special effort is required to sing praises. Whereas the frog is never in any such quandary.

A creature lacking intelligent awareness is also saved from the sins of self-consciousness. In human life, of course, this self-consciousness is a necessary principle; every child has to learn it from the very start. Afterward, there are cultural values that enhance the sense of the ego. Not that this is to be seen as some basic human weakness; it is a fundamental part of Creation. Even a saint has to feel that he exists; even the person who loves God with all his heart and devotes his entire being to God has to have a self to offer up. One cannot escape the need of man to possess his own soul. It is merely the insistence on this consciousness of oneself, so largely a matter of education and ideology, that is questionable. The extreme case is that of the closed circle of the self-sufficient ego. The problem of the self, then, is applicable to all living things. Even the angels. Men are able to struggle against it somehow, but the angels, poor creatures, remain as they are, unable to grow and unable to learn more than what they know. For the angel knows that it has a self, but this identity, no matter how loaded with sanctity, is not entirely nullified before God. Which puts the angel in a position of questionable superiority to man, who can at least attempt to repudiate himself before God.

This self-disavowal before God, the repudiation of one's separateness, is not only a theoretical concept, it has become a very practical principle in Chasidism, especially in the Chabad school. There is a story, told as a joke, about a Chasid who, after an inspiring lesson in Chasidism, wandered about at the edge of the castle grounds (of a Polish aristocrat), where he was accosted by a sentinel who called out: "Who goes there?" Still under the impression of what he had learned, the Chasid answered: "It is I who go." And when the sentinel demanded to know who "I" was, the Chasid said: "That which is null and void goes." "Who is that?" inquired the perplexed soldier. Upon which the Chasid thought to himself: "It seems that this fellow recognizes that something or someone still remains; evidently, my self-negation has not been complete enough." So he answered: "There is no going. That which is null and void can't be said to go."

Just as we cannot grasp the concept of Creation— it is no more than a matter of words for most of us—so are we baffled by the idea of Tzimtzum. To be sure, we can speak of it and say that it is an explanation of existence. But all we are saying is that only that which is infinite can conceal the infinite, which is necessarily all-pervasive. And the problem is not merely a theoretical one; it spills over into the problems of good and evil, light and dark. . . . Because just as God is to be found in Creation, in that which is good, He is also to be found in the opposite of existence, in the negation of life, as well. As in the saying by the sages: May the good bless Thee, oh Lord; but why should not the evil also bless Thee! To be sure, we may claim that it is impossible for the evil to bless God. On the other hand, we cannot offer up to God only the good, even if we do wish to relate the good and the light to Him and to disclaim the rest.

It is like the interdependence of Chesed and Gevurah. Both are manifestations of the Divine, not one as positive manifestation and the other as its negative counterpart, but both as equally representing some aspect of the Divine. They are connected in that a Divine revelation of kindness and generosity is accompanied by an equal revelation in terms of Divine restriction and concealment. In which case it is not darkness (or ignorance) that reveals or indicates the Divine, but the act of his concealment—for "I am the Lord who hides His face." It is an act of manifestation just as much as "I am the Lord who speaks and acts" or "I am the Lord who rewards deeds of kindness." Both aspects, then, are equal as manifestations.

There is something of this sort in the *Sefer Yetzirah* (The Book of Creation), where it is said: The good distinguishes evil and evil distinguishes good. They are the two aspects of one picture. Or else, as it is asked: Which part of the written letter is the sign—the black mark or the white space around it? Which part is the reality—that which is or that which is not? It is not merely a problem of logic or metaphysics. It is connected with our problem concerning the essence of the world. What makes the world, the darkness or the light, the concealment or the revelation?

As the Sages said: The Torah was given in black fire against white fire. The point being that the Torah is not in either the black or the white fire; it is in the one against the background of the other. This is true of all scripture. The writing is itself holy, as is the parchment. Because when holiness enters, it pervades the whole entity. Sometimes the page can be holier than the writing; it all depends on the circumstance. In any case, the relation between the black and the white is the relation between two realities, both of them equally valid as actual being. Sometimes the form of the letter is a matter of the spacing, sometimes the important thing is the color or the darkness, as in an engraving, where the letter consists of "that which is not" in terms of form and actual substance. Or in an imperfect mirror, where the black is an absence of reflecting material.

What is being said here is that the Divine darkness should not be avoided, because He exists in absence as well as presence, in the evil as in the good. For instance, in praying for the dead, we say: Blessed be He who judges in Truth. The same prayer is spoken to confirm that God is present in any special situation—when one sees something of His goodness or revelation, something in the nature of a miracle. Thus, "Baruch Dayan Emet" (Blessed is He who judges or decides all things in Truth) declares a sort of Divine manifestation. You God, who have been revealed in this particular moment of decision, You who are concealed in the judgment, are made manifest. I bless the revelation of God in the darkness.

The hiddenness of God, His concealment, is no more than a vessel or an instrument to contain the light given it by some form or other. Indeed, one may see the creation of the world itself as a matter of Din—Judgment—and not only Mercy or Kindness, because it involves the concealment of God and not His revelation. What is required in Creation is the power to give form, to put limits and fix boundaries to all things and processes. It is not only the power to manifest abundance and life-force. As for the vessels to contain all this, they have to be varied, as speech is, and composed of the basic letters of Creation. Every such letter is a fundamental vessel of Creation; it is not itself the light of Creation, it is the light within a particular vessel of Creation.

And when we speak of the letter—we mean the spoken letter. Which brings us to consider what we mean by speech. Speech is formed out of two essential components: the vowel ejaculation that provides volume and sound, and the consonantal restriction of sound by lips, throat, and tongue. Of the twenty-two letters of the alphabet, each of which is an essence in itself, there are five that are also "terminal" letters—having a special form at the end of a word—that are restraining, Gevurah factors. The letter *mem* at the end of a word is not the same as a *mem* in the middle of a word, where it still has sound momentum and continuity. The terminal letters symbolize, and correspond to, the five restraining forces that are half of the ten Sefirot. (The Sefirot are charted as a figure with a right and a left side, the right being related to Chesed and the left to Gevurah.) The five Gevurah Sefirot afterward create those letters that in their combinations, are the basis of the Creation.

The Kabbalah mentions the "light from the dark," a term delineating a point of illumination, like a candle that lights up the whole surrounding darkness and represents the first or highest level of being, called the "Atik Yomin" (Ancient of Days). In another context, it is known as the inwardness of Keter, or the Crown, the sense of bliss in the Will, which is the quality of all beginning. But "Ancient of Days" is also considered the candle that fashions the darkness, that which is the ground for the Divine act of Tzimtzum, withdrawal or contraction of the darkness in order for a form of light to appear and make the world possible. In order for there to be a world, there has to be a "Light from the Dark" that will hide the Divine light—otherwise there can be no individual things separate from Him.

As for the source of the Divine benevolence, it is also in the "Ancient of Days"—the infinite giving and the infinite concealment are both part of the primary act of Creation. In order to understand the apparent contradiction, let us realize that the withdrawal of God, the concealment, can be the most terrible thing of all if one does not know what it is. Only when a man knows that it is a voluntary and necessary withdrawal of Divine presence can he accept it.

It has been argued that it is easy enough to accept Divine judgment, no matter how difficult, so long as it does not touch one directly. When it strikes others, one can call it a conceal-ment of God—He is hiding His face, and it has to be accepted with joy as something ordained by Divine wisdom. But when it strikes oneself, when it strikes in such a way that not only is the good taken away, but a person is deprived of the power to bear the evil—then this is even worse than the evil itself.

There is a saying that a complete Tzadik, or Saint, is the one who is favored by the good. Because a saint is someone who is convinced that everything happens (to him) for the best. It is not that he is the sort of person who cannot suffer, let us say, objectively; it is just that he cannot suffer subjectively. He is happy with his lot because he does not see the hiddenness of God. To him, there is Chesed (Mercy) and there is Gevurah (Judgment), like the right arm and the left arm of Divinity, and when God touches him, what does it matter whether He does so with His right hand or His left.

This is a high level of spiritual awareness, of course, but it is common enough in prayers such as the Hallel, where one says, "I will sing for there is Mercy and Judgment; I will rejoice in God both in Salvation and in trouble." This is a power of seeing clearly, of being able to see that He who hides His face is the same one as He who shows His face. So that this apparent duality of Chesed and Gevurah is really a unity and becomes a fundamental principle of existence in human life. One learns that the concealment is also the revelation of God—in other terms, in other colors.

The truth is that we are always in a situation of confession, whether it is the Day of Atonement (Yom Kippur) or the midnight prayer of "Kriyat Shema"—and we ask Him to erase our sins, not by pain and suffering but—if He does not mind—by forgiveness and mercy. It does not always work out; we are not always given what we ask for, at least in the manner or at the time we want it. But actually, all that happens, the good and the evil, are aspects of His manifestation. Except that our recognition is limited to those moments when we know that it is so. At such times the situation is altogether different. One can relate differently, not that there is less pain and suffering: it is merely that there is not that feeling of the concealment of His countenance. So long as He is not altogether absent, we can accept all that happens to us.

5

Breaking through the Barrier

It is written that at first God thought to create the world completely under the sign of judgment, or law. This meant that He Himself would be completely absent—everything would proceed according to its own nature and there would be no need for Divine interference. Such a world would be sealed and finished; there would be no way of anything getting beyond itself. But God saw that this was not feasible, that it was necessary for mercy to be able to operate in the world, not only as a form of being, but manifesting as revelation. Something had to penetrate the hard core, even if only as a flash of light that would illuminate the darkness of deterministic density. This, incidentally, is the image used by the Rambam to describe the nature of prophecy: It is like what happens to a man walking in utter darkness. Suddenly there is a flash of lightning, which, for a moment, shows him where he is, so that afterward, even though he is still in darkness, he has at least oriented himself and knows where he has to go. This is also an illustration of the collaboration between the attribute of Gevurah and the attribute of Chesed to bring about revelation.

Concerning revelation, there are two ways in which it takes

place. One is through men of God, Tzadikim on all the levels of their appearance down the ages: as patriarchs, prophets, sages, and the like. The other is the "signs and wonders" of the Bible that are direct revelations and whose peak is the giving of the Torah.

Tzadikim, as defined by the Baal HaTanya in another context, are those extraordinary men, not necessarily outstanding as good or saintly—although this may be a condition for their mission—who represent a sort of higher human being. Yet, the Tzadik is not simply someone on a higher level. Superiority in itself does not make the Tzadik, and one does not become a Tzadik by improving oneself, except perhaps in very exceptional cases. A person is born a Tzadik. Which does not mean that even if one is born that way, one has to be a Tzadik. Indeed, almost everyone is born with a talent, a gift, or inclination for a certain task, whether one uses it or not. So that a person can remain only a potential genius or prophet all his life. As for the one born with this genius to recognize the Divine, he can then experience and know far more about spiritual matters than an ordinary person who yearns and strives all his life for precisely this sort of thing. But, as said, it depends on what one does with it. Not in vain has there been so much talk of the hidden Tzadikim, by virtue of whom the world continues to exist. These are the Tzadikim who, although they live in the world, do not work in the world. Enough that such a person just be somewhere, as a humble cobbler or even as a leader of his people, just so long as he is hidden. There is the story of the son of a famous Rabbi who asked his father: Why do the Tzadikim have to be hidden away somewhere? And the Rabbi answered: And do you think that the revealed Tzadikim are precisely what we see of them? So, too, a hidden Tzadik can be concealed, not only in apparent ignorance or in obscurity of position. He can be concealed in the very task of leadership or within the function of a famous Tzadik. His hiddenness lies in the quality of his relationship to this world and to that which is beyond this world.

Thus a Tzadik is not usually recognized by the world, nor does he make contact with the world except with one aspect of his being; at another extreme, he does not belong at all to the reality of the world. Which does not mean that there is a split in personality. On the contrary, as the example of a graphological study of the handwriting of the Baal HaTanya shows, a complete harmony and unification of personality seems to be one of the most notable characteristics of a Tzadik. One can even feel something of this quality in this book, with its understanding of the pains and weaknesses of man. The Tzadik understands the pain, but it is not from within; it is as though he grasps it all from outside. He comprehends that a person may sin, but it seems to him rather odd, like the observations of a researcher of a strange species. One has the impression that there is some such relationship. Which in turn may serve to hint at the nature of the hidden within the manifest, how a person may be far above and beyond what he reveals to the world.

Briefly, what is being stated is that the Tzadikim are the spearheads of the manifestation of being within the nothingness. This is also true, for instance, of the signs and wonders of the Torah, which are sent in order to help mankind. The task of the Tzadik is to point out and, when necessary, to function as a window to the world of real being, just as the miracle serves the same purpose of a corridor or passageway, or rather of a momentary access to a wider existence.

In our world of Action (Asiyah), as in the upper worlds of Formation (Yetzirah) and Creation (Briah), there is a difference between the subject and object, between that which acts and that which is acted upon. Whereas, in the highest world, that of Emanation (Atzilut), where the Sefirot are not separate from their source in the Godhead, this difference does not exist. All things in the lower worlds are thus able to be distinct; even the Angel in the World of Briah, who is a perfect instrument of the Divine, is still a creature with an "I." It is only in the World of Emanation that there are no partitions between Creator and created, and God and His world are one. Consequently, whatever we can distinguish in any way, no matter how great, is not God.

Even Moses, the man who rose higher than any other, was unable to penetrate the world of Atzilut (Emanation). "No man shall see Me and live" (Exodus 33:20). Revelation is thus not a visual confrontation with anything in the World of Emanation; it is a matter of seeing truth from behind, so to speak, or below, through the veil of the lower Worlds of Briah, Yetzirah, and Asiyah. What is more, revelation has to be clothed or wrapped in the lower attributes like Netzach, Hod, Yesod, which is the only way even prophets, such as Moses, can grasp it. Even the higher attributes, like Chesed and Gevurah, cannot be properly grasped except through these lower ones, especially through Yesod (the Tzadik).

What do the Tzadikim do in Paradise? The Talmud suggests that they sit with their diadems on their heads and enjoy the bliss of the Holy Shechinah (*Brachot* 17a). The essence of Paradise could then be seen as an extension of the Divine illumination experienced in this life. The achievement itself is Paradise. And that is the uniqueness of the human soul—that it can achieve such a unity which is the essence of Paradise. It involves Chesed and Gevurah, which are called the nourishment of the Tzadik. The differentiation is here made between that which nourishes and that which clothes the living soul. It is also the relation between the inner light and the outer, or transcendental, light. When, in physical or spiritual terms, I experience something in the nature of nourishment, I imbibe it by swallowing it into myself. The other way of responding to a revelation is by putting it on, clothing and covering myself with it as a garment. Such expressions occur frequently enough in the Bible, such as: in Proverbs—Go and eat of my bread and drink of the wine of my wisdom; or in Isaiah—And he shall put on righteousness (as a mantle); or the symbolic description of Ezekiel eating the scrolls.

Thus, there can be said to be two kinds of conceptual grasp: one—impressionistic, inclusive, atmospheric, and intuitive—that cannot be analyzed and broken up into components, and another—more intellectual and conscious comprehension—given to analysis and explanation. The first includes influences that are not always conscious, but may be very powerful and meaningful. This internal one is of the nature of the "food" of the Tzadikim. The other, more outer, is the "garment" of the Tzadikim.

A firmament is something that covers, envelops, and serves

as a curtain. It is likened to the Torah because the Torah is also a combination of the revealed and the hidden, and because if the Torah were to speak in the language of God, it would be too much for us in terms of joy and splendor, and we would be consumed by it. We can come in contact with the Torah only because it is wrapped in metaphors and symbols, one within another. The Torah is called the primordial metaphor, the paradigm of the world prior to its creation. To some, the Torah is seen enveloped in veils and mysteries, as was mentioned, written in black fire on white fire, expressing the infinite complexity of revelation within the hidden, the relation of darkness and light, with the reader never absolutely certain which is which.

Fire is one of the symbols for the left side of the chart of the Sefirot, and of Gevurah in particular, expressing the power of annihilation and destruction that puts an end or limit to something. So that whereas water is the corresponding symbol for the right side, the source of the fire of the Torah is the result also of the combination of both sides, Chesed and Gevurah (Mercy and Justice). As for the firmament, here betokening the secret of the Torah, it is beyond the grasp even of Tzadikim in Paradise. Because, after all, what is a Tzadik in Paradise? It is a higher state of being, the result of the liberation from the body, which binds one to sensual and mental experiences, and from all that the soul experienced when it was still in the body.

Even so, these Tzadikim in Paradise cannot know the secret of the Torah; they can only contain it within themselves. For Paradise is not the world of the secret of the Torah, it is the world of the secret of secrets. While we are on earth we need the firmament, which is an envelope of mystery, and from this visible firmament there drips the dew food for the soul, or Torah. It is an image that is repeated often enough in the Bible and elsewhere. All this dew or food for the soul is also the secret of the twenty-two letters of the Torah.

The Tzadik does not himself dwell in the firmament; he receives the dew or spiritual nourishment from the firmament, which is the secret of knowledge. And this knowledge is the higher knowledge that is beyond human comprehension. Which is one of the reasons why it is said that there is no rest for the Tzadikim, who continue to progress from one level to another—even in Paradise, where the secret of knowledge ceases to be secret, for even then mystery, the essence of secrecy, remains. For one cannot ever get beyond the secret of the infinite. One progresses from firmament to firmament; always there are new skies above one's head, whether in this world or the next.

There is no study of Torah without some degree of higher consciousness. To a corresponding degree, and in some specific way or other, too, the Torah is thus internalized. So that Torah is always that which is here called food. At the same time, there are two aspects to Torah. On one hand, it is itself a mitzvah. There is the mitzvah to study, the command of "Limud Torah," even if only to repeat certain words. The other aspect is the interiorization, that which relates to consciousness and comprehension, so that Torah is called food. It is nourishment in this life and food for the soul in the next life, the difference being that in this life, there is no way of knowing to what extent the soul is being fed by Torah. Such is Torah, while the mitzvot are always garments. The mitzvah is not a matter of the mind; it is an action. The mitzvah is measured and delineated by the way in which one does something and not by the degree of consciousness involved. The degree of comprehension may be considered rather a reflection of the amount of Torah involved.

When one probes the question of which is preferable, Torah or mitzvot, the answer is usually ambivalent. Torah, or study, is usually thought to be preferred to mitzvot, or action, because study brings right action, a conclusion that only leaves the problem open to further analysis. If study is preferred only because it brings action, then obviously action is the more important side of the coin. On the other hand, one may give many interpretations to the preference for study and many shades of meaning to the reason for the preference. One returns to the problem of the various kinds of revelation and which is better, that which is conscious or that which is above and beyond consciousness. For example: Should one study only those parts of the Torah whose meaning one understands, and the more one understands the greater the progress made?

The alternate is the doing of mitzvah, with or without understanding, like tefillin, which can be performed with a greater or
lesser comprehension. To be sure, there is that much more
enjoyment to be gained by increase of understanding and
knowing. But in actuality, one wraps oneself in the mitzvah as
in a garment. So that it has been said that the mitzvot
(commandments) as a whole form the clothes of Tzadikim, and
these garments are woven by the strands of the individual
mitzvah performances into a completer whole, a seamless
mantle, as it is called in the *Zohar*. There are many folk tales
that tell about the way a holy person can weave a garment of
this sort for himself, and the way a part of this garment, such
as a sleeve, may be missing because of some persistent error in
the performance of a mitzvah.

What we are attempting to clarify here belongs more to the
human experience than to philosophical thought. Having considered the relationship between being and nonbeing, between
Creation and the problems of God's hiddenness, we are
confronted with the reality of the miraculous and the holy, the
meaning of Torah and mitzvot in the immense unity of the
cosmos. For these manifestations of the spirit constitute something that breaks through the barrier between God and the
world. But since God Himself created the barrier, this concealment of Himself as a necessary function of infinite existence, it
was not meant to be broken through. Man can try to penetrate
the wall as much as he likes, and he does sometimes bash his
head to an astonishing degree, until he is certain he sees sparks
and light of a Divine radiance, but it is all in vain. To be sure,
there are those few who find what they consider a crack or a
peephole and make much of it.

It is here maintained, however, that the only reliable and
fixed apertures to the Divine are Torah and mitzvot. Of course,
even these openings are obscure because we ourselves are slow
to seize the opportunity they offer, and because it is far too
dangerous to let too much light through. Nevertheless, men do
experience something in their souls, even if what is revealed is
usually only external, in the nature of the transcendental.
Nevertheless, sometimes there is a release from the sensual,
from the hiddenness of the apparent, and man can perceive a
deeper reality, like the "dew that drips from the firmament and

provides nourishment for the souls in Paradise." In order to attain an appreciable degree of such perception, there is needed a great divestment of the physical in terms of love of God—at which stage a stone is no longer a different object: it is a different condition. The next world is another level of being, not another place. A person can pierce through to this stage, if only in a momentary flash of enlightenment, but it is still not a vision of God. It is, rather, a passing look out of the surrounding darkness into a mist that gives the impression of better visibility.

6

The Higher Meaning of Gevurah

The name *Elokim*, which is one of the names of God, refers to the attribute of Gevurah, or, to be more precise, it is the name of that Divine manifestation that is revealed through the attribute of Gevurah. For the name of God cannot be identical with the name of an attribute, which is that through which God reveals something of Himself. The connection with Nature is through the same Tzimtzum (contraction) aspect of this revelation, with its creation of the laws of existence. The Ineffable Name, or Tetragrammaton, Havayah (YHVH), God as eternal being, denotes that manifestation that is not a single event, but is ongoing and constant, creating at every moment. We need the concept of Nature to keep things within categories, to indicate the Divine absence that allows specific things to exist as though by themselves. In fact, nature is only the general name we have given to a system of relatively stable harmony. It is a concept common to all languages and cultures, with its closely integrated concept of law, or rather natural law, because nature is, in actuality, no more than the inclusive system of repetitive patterns. The fact of this steady and reliable repetition hides the Divine reality behind it; we see a law of nature and not a creative act of God.

70

The sun can be relied upon to rise every day as it has for so long in the past. It is the unusual and the unnatural that makes man become aware of the Divine. So that the unpredictable behavior of human beings becomes a matter for speculation about God as well as a problem for scientists.

However, the world only seems to carry on by itself in a fixed and stable manner. It is made possible by the shield and covering provided by Gevurah and denoted as *Elokim*. But, as we have said, there are other aspects to the concealment. Part of it is to allow for the action of free choice, because if one sees the Divine face to face, it is impossible to deny Him. (It may be that it would also be impossible to sin, but this requires some investigation. Could it be that people would get so accustomed to God, as they do to everything else, that they would even commit transgression before Him?) In any case, the existence of God in terms of revelation is not given to denial. It is the other side of the concealment, the first side being the fact that if God exists, how can there be a world in any way separate from Him, not nullified by Him? As it is written (Malachi 3:6), "I am Havaya, that which is and never changes." As though to ask: And you, Israel (or the world as a whole), have you not been dissolved (in my light)? And the answer is that the concealment of the Divine name hides the aspect of Havayah, the aspect of Divine Being in all His manifestations, and permits His creatures to exist and not to be automatically nullified and wiped out.

Clearly, then, that which we call Gevurah, Tzimtzum, or Divine Hiddenness is not entirely negation. Not only is it not a complete darkness and a void, but it contains its own grace, its own power to save, because otherwise the original Chesed of Divine manifestation would destroy the substance of the world with its light. It is possible, therefore, to speak of an attribute of giving and plenty (Chesed), which saves by restraining, hiding, or limiting Divine power, and the opposite, a concealment, contraction, or Tzimtzum, which works benevolently.

In other words, we cannot consider the Sefirot or attributes as blind forces, like those of nature; they are each of them self-motivating, each functioning within itself and purposeful in its action. Nevertheless, they are not isolated and structurally separate. On the contrary, Gevurah can be a vehicle of Chesed and Chesed can be an instrument of Gevurah. It is essential for them to work in combination in order for the world to exist. They are bound to one another at the root, growing out of the same source, and there is no essential contradiction between them.

We seem to be touching on the idea behind certain contradictory phrases such as: "I form the light and the darkness. I make peace and create evil" (Isaiah 45:7). The common factor in this notion of the same God making both good and evil is not to deny that they are separate and opposite elements. Each operates separately, has its own rules and guidelines, and is in essential opposition to the other. The fact that Gevurah can be a vessel for Chesed only shows that both grow out of the same root. In human life, too, one can point to such combinations of Chesed and Gevurah being channels for one another. If parents give children all they desire, as an act of Chesed, this benevolence (spoiling the children) can turn into a great evil, a concealment of Divine grace. On the other hand, the response to an act of punishment can be one of grace and goodness, Chesed, not only in terms of results, but even in terms of feeling. It has been sarcastically remarked, for instance, that the punishment of the serpent in the Garden of Eden was really a great gift, because if he can live from the dust of the earth, he doesn't have to strive to make a living—he has all that he requires and lacks nothing. The answer to this is that this is precisely the forcefulness of the judgment of God upon the serpent: I give you all the food in the world to eat, and you can go to perdition—I do not want you to turn to me for anything more. So that the Gevurah aspect of Chesed and the Chesed aspect of Gevurah are very much interwoven and interdependent. Everything in our world is a combination. The attributes grow out of one root, and there is no such thing in man as a pure manifestation of Gevurah or Chesed or any other attribute. Each manifestation is mixed. In nature, of course, it is different, and we readily distinguish between specific forces of attraction and repulsion and the like, and observe how objects change their location and creatures their habits according to definite, if blind, mechanical influences.

The essence of faith is that Havayah (YHVH) is *Elokim* (God), and that both of them are indeed one. And it is not a matter of the same thing having two names; they are two different modes of Divine manifestation. Similarly, it is written, for example, that one should say blessings for the evil that befalls one as well as for the good. What is more, one should do so in the same way, with the same sincerity. Because in blessing, one is praising God, glorifying Him, and when one says, "Blessed art Thou, Whose actions and judgments are true," in response to some fateful blow, the meaning has to be accepted in the same way as "Thou who brings the evening." In other words, just as one blesses the inevitable darkness of evening, one has to bless evil; there is a fixed blessing for each. And when one blesses in this way, the implication is that one is able to receive the aspect of *Elokim* (as Gevurah) within Chesed and that this, too, is a Divine revelation. Perhaps it would be too much to call it a revelation, seeing that it is more in the nature of manifestation through concealment. It is the other side of the miraculous manifestation through Divine revelation. In neither case is it a matter of God's absence, but rather of different forms of His presence—in darkness as in light, in evil as in good.

In fact, the only kind of evil that has no blessing at all is the human evil, sheer malevolence or badness. This is the real concealment of the Divine countenance, God's absence. Human evil is the hiddenness of the face of God in the sense that one does not see Him. To illustrate, there are pure animals and unclean animals listed in the scripture. The unclean beasts are not evil in any way whatsoever; the pig is not bad as a pig and becomes bad only when I eat it, upon which it is transformed into evil in an absolute sense. Before that, it wasn't anything better or worse than any other of God's creatures. The only real evil is that which is created by man, when man destroys or damages the order of God.

Upon which, we find ourselves somehow touching upon the problem of death—or at least the very human problem of death as evil. According to the various scriptural commentaries, we may gather that death is a severance of the soul from the body. It can be a phenomenon that is a part of the universal reality, or it can be considered a part of the reality that is evil. There are differences of opinion about this, even on the highest levels, but that is not the point. The issue we are confronting is how this severance of soul from body takes place—whether it is done by the Angel of Death or by God. Of course, we may presume that every person must die, that the Angel of Death comes to all men.

This makes death the ultimate evil, the very essence of evil as evil, and yet it does not stem from the fact that the soul ceases to dwell in the body, but rather from the fact that death is an expression of all the evil in existence. Which is perhaps the reason for the verses in the Psalms (6:4, 16:10) asking the Lord to save me from Death (Sheol). The rather perplexing thing here is that God should rescue me from death. After all, one must die. What evil is there to save one from? There are a great number of explanations, for instance, to the notion that Moses did not die, that he was taken up by God, or that Jacob did not experience death. There was a separation perhaps of body and soul—in Moses' case there was the "kiss of death," a clinging of the soul to the Divine. For an ordinary mortal, death is that moment of contact with the essence of evil in the form of the annihilation of life; that is, it is more than concealment—it is the absence of Divinity, the nothing. This, incidentally, explains the difference in the points of view concerning the halachic problem of the nature of the influences present at the tombs of Tzadikim, the idea being that, though dead and the very source of uncleanness, nevertheless the Tzadik, even in death, does not defile, because there is a difference between the death of a Tzadik and the death of an ordinary man. In the case of common mortals, death is the utmost evil, as said, whereas for a Tzadik, death is a cause for rejoicing on earth. What is being stated here, then, is that evil is not something absolute in itself—it is something that is made what it is, either directly or indirectly, by man himself. Because evil is the man-made vacuum, the very opposite of Divine manifestation, which is necessarily good in all its forms. The Lord (Havayah) is God in all possible aspects.

What, then, is the meaning of "there is nothing else"? After all, the earth is solid and real enough, unlike living things that give indication of something else that animates them and gives them substance. So that matter would seem to be basic, the fundamental reality upon which all else is built. Nevertheless, even matter does not have an existence of its own apart from the existence of God.

As said, the name *Elokim* is the concealment of the name Havayah, but it does not necessarily mean that it itself is hidden. Just as I can cover one hand by another hand, hiding it from view by others, even though I myself can see it quite clearly. The concealment is, therefore, not at all fictitious, even though it has no such meaning for me. The reason is that both hands are mine, and there is no appreciable significance in the covering of any one by the other. For anyone else, it might be meaningful. The anyone else (as far as God is concerned)— the lower orders of being—thus live in the concealment, and the contents of their lives emerge from the relation between the hidden and the manifest.

The different names of God are also different attributes; they are not various ways of saying the same thing. And they do not indicate any sort of differences or contradictions within the being of the Divine. In a way, then, it seems as though God functions anonymously. For those who do not know His name, this anonymity is decisive. For He who is the Creator and the bearer of the name, it does not matter by which name He is called.

In fact, when we say the Lord (Havayah) is *Elokim*, the intention is to remove this barrier and the concealment stemming from the name *Elokim*. We add that He and His Name are one to emphasize that there is no difference between God and *Elokim*.

"The Lord is God in the heavens above and on the earth below; there is nothing else" (Deuteronomy 4:39). By which is meant that the world does not exist as something specific, separate, and additional to God, not only in the sense of something whole, but also in the sense of an accretion, a sort of afterthought. For the heavens above and the earth below is all there is; there is no such thing as "something else." Another explanation concerning the meaning of *od*, of something else, is that the soul is the human being and the body is the *od*. The body is the "something else" of the soul. Such, for instance, was the explanation given to the passage (Psalm 146:2): "I will praise the Lord with my life, I will sing psalms to my God with my being (*odi*)." Praising the Lord with my life is the expression of the living soul; singing to God also with my being, my something else (*odi*), is the expression of my body. In other words, it is a song of the soul and the body, in which they are like the sun and that which shields from the burning of the sun, like the Divine manifestation and its concealment.

Now, why do we say that in the heavens above and in the earth below there is nothing else (but God), and why have we said that the something else is the accretion to the soul? For concerning the soul it cannot be said that there is nothing else, because there is something else. But, as far as God is concerned, the world is "nothing else." The reason for this is the fact that the relation between the body and the soul is not the same as the relation between the world and God, even though this metaphor appears in various writings. At any rate, the metaphor may help us to understand certain things, but it is not entirely correct. For in spite of the interdependence of body and soul, the soul does not actualize the body—it merely animates it, supports it, drives it. The body has its own sort of vitality, independent of the soul; when the soul departs and the body remains, at least for a while the body does not disappear.

On the other hand, one cannot continue to hold on to the light without the source of light. One cannot hold on to the picture without the material on which it is formed. So that, since God not only gives life to the world, but God constitutes the world in essence, it may be said that He creates His own existence. Which means that the world has no reality at all without the Divine light, and the fact that there is a Divine light that appears to be separate from the world is only because that is one of the ways in which Creation manifests. The creation of the world is itself an image, a metaphor, and, therefore, very much a matter of language. As it is written: ". . . like the grasshopper whose garment is from himself and is himself." I observe that there is a garment—an appearance—and an inner reality. But they are not two separate existences; one cannot be in the world without the other. They are both one essence, but they do not manifest it the same way, even though they are derived from the same root and one cannot exist without the other.

The soul does not create the body out of nothing; the body is formed from something else that exists in the world and develops according to the laws of life. The body is thus something in itself; it is not a function of the soul, even if it is controlled by the soul. Creation, however, is from Divine light directly and is continuous. The sun did not create light at some time or other and send it out; it keeps on creating and illuminating all the time. The fact of sunlight is an ongoing process that continues, and there is no possibility of its existence without the sun.

The Divine concealment is intended to support the idea that the world exists as an actuality on all its levels and manifestations. This concealment, or Gevurah, is not something additional, as though to hide something else, like a veil over Creation. On the contrary, the Lord is God (Havayah is *Elokim*), and since this is so, the concealment itself is of the same stuff as the revelation. The Divine hiddenness and the Divine manifestation are both revelations, except that one is a white fire and the other is a black fire. And from both together, whose essence is from God, the existence of the world takes form and develops.

7

The Paradox of World and God

In the *Zohar* (I:18b), it is written that the verse, "Hear O Israel, the Lord is our God, the Lord is One" (Deuteronomy 6:4) is a higher level of unity, while the verse that follows it in the daily prayers, "Blessed is the name of the glory of His Kingdom forever and ever," is a lower level of unity. Indeed, they are the two sides of the same thing, two aspects or points of view of the one matter, and the letters can even be mixed to form a certain wholeness.

It may well be asked: What is the reason for such a paradox? Why does God have to keep Himself hidden so that we see only a world and do not see Him? The answer is that the very purpose of Creation is Revelation. True, the world was formed by the act of Divine withdrawal, God's concealing Himself to make room for something else to exist, but it was done in order to make some higher union possible. In Kabbalistic terms, the point of Creation was the final phase, the attribute, or Sefirah, of Malchut (Kingdom). That is, there is no king without a kingdom, no sovereign without a people to rule over. The other attributes are more or less self-sufficient; Chesed or Loving-kindness, for example, does not need anyone around to be good to in order to be itself. But Malchut is not self-sufficient;

there is no kingship without a people—sovereignty cannot exist by itself. Therefore, in order for God to reveal Himself, He had to create a people. It would not be enough to create children, no matter how numerous, for a father cannot be a king; what is more, a king rules over that which is not himself in the sense that even his lords and ministers do not constitute a kingdom. A certain real distance or separation as well as active involvement is necessary between ruler and people. The name of God (Lord) that expresses this particular qualification is known as Adnut.

On the other hand, the name of God (YHVH) known as Havayah may be considered to belong to that realm of existence that is beyond the reality of the world as we know it. Nevertheless, there is something we call an amalgamation of Havayah and the name Adnut expressing the unity of the two worlds.

As has been said, in terms of time and space, reality is nullified before God, like the light of the sun in the sun itself— and this is known as higher-level unity, also called the integration of the name Adnut in the name Havayah. The other side of this is that even though the Divine is above time and space, He is, nevertheless, present in time and in space—and this is the lower-level unity, the integration of Havayah in Adnut. Thus Yichudah Ila'ah (Higher Unity) is, technically, the integration of Adnut with Havayah; Yichudah Tate'ah (Lower Unity) is the integration of Havayah with Adnut. In writing, the letters of the two names alternate to make one (unpronounceable) name. To be sure, these integrations are technical symbols, trying to depict something of the intermingling of Higher Unity and Lower Unity.

But what is the difference between them? Havayah, as has been explained, is Divine existence before which the real world is nullified into absolute nothingness. The integration of Adnut with Havayah, which is Higher Unity, means that time and space and all reality are cancelled in the same way. Thus, just as in Havayah, there is nothing besides Him, so time and space and reality, which are manifestations of Adnut, are nullified when Adnut is integrated with Havayah in Higher Unity. On the other hand, Lower Unity is within space and time, integrating Havayah, which is also Ein Sof (Infinite), into the world of reality.

To be sure, these are only technical devices in defining the compounding of Divine existence with the reality of the world and may be considered two aspects of the same thing. Which is not to say that there is no real difference between Higher Unity and Lower Unity. If we approach the matter from another angle, another viewpoint, considering, as in the prayer of Hannah, that "The Lord is a God of all knowledge" (I Samuel 2:3), we may ask: What is the meaning of knowledge? There is higher knowledge and lower knowledge, the knowledge God has of the world and the knowledge the world has of God. The higher knowledge is that which sees the world as though from God's viewpoint, in which case the world is no longer real. The lower knowledge sees God's view of the world through the eyes of the world, in which case there is a reality—a reality through which, at the same time, one sees God, the transcendental. Now these two conceptual modes may be maintained separately, or they can be fused and be considered two aspects of the same thing—or rather one the reverse of the other in the way certain mirrors can be made to have two sides, one surface reflecting and the other side, not opaque, but transparent. In which case, the difference between the real world and the nonexistent world is a matter of which direction one is looking. It is the barrier, whether mirror or window, between the World of Emanation and the World of Creation. This, then, is also the difference between Higher Unity and Lower Unity, whether one sees through everything, as though all were transparent, or whether one sees things as dense, opaque, altogether impenetrable, as only one-way passages. From this point of view, we should apprehend the world as being both invisible and visible at the same time, depending on which direction one looks at it.

We have not ventured as yet into the human aspects of the question, besides the recognition that Higher Unity means a repudiation of the world. In Lower Unity, the world is accepted as it is, and one tries to see the ways of God in it.

The fundamental problem—human as well as philosophical—is that if the "Shema Yisrael" declaration is Higher Unity, then how is it possible to say, immediately afterwards, as the daily prayers enjoin one to say, "And thou shalt love the Lord thy God with all thy heart and with all thy soul and with all thy being."? This question, which has its own history in Chasidic thought, has been answered by the Baal HaTanya in a way that has some bearing on the problem of relationship between the two levels of Divine union. There has to be, he said, something in the nature of Lower Unity between the two declarations of faith. This is usually accomplished by the silent statement, "Blessed is the Name of the Glory of His Kingdom," and without it, one cannot reach the aspired for unity. The point being that Lower Unity, amongst other things, consists of seeing the Infinite by way of the world. In other words, even though the Infinite Light is above time and place, it is also below them because the lowest Sefirah, Kingdom (Malchut), which is the source of time and place, is itself united with the Infinite Light. The focal point of the perception obtained by Lower Unity is the objective reality of the world, not the denial of the world but the objective reality of a world within which the infinite exists.

This light of the Infinite (Ein Sof) is thus not to be found beyond the world; one cannot really speak of anything that has no place, even the light of Ein Sof. At the same time, one cannot say that God is to be found above, in the heavens; it is patently absurd and fit only for atheists to speculate on. There can be no direction to God's being—above or below in any meaningful way as far as geography is concerned; it can only be in terms of levels, in the sense of different planes of existence. Only thus can it be said that the dimension of Ein Sof is above and beyond the world. To be sure, this other-worldly dimension has become, in a manner of speaking, the point of departure for those philosophies that maintain that, since Ein Sof or God is beyond the world, then there is no connection between them, and there is an essential, unbridgeable gap between Divinity and reality as we know it. However, when, in our prayers, we say, "He who is in the heavens above and in the earth below," the meaning is that everything is full of the Ein Sof, equally in all its parts.

Even though the Divine attribute of Malchut is the source of the existence of the world, it is not in any way separate from God. Even in the framework of time and space, the light of Ein Sof clothes the attribute of Malchut. Therefore, the truth that there is no one besides Him does not only mean that there is no other power or divinity possible, but that there is no other reality. Even the reality of time and place and existence indicate His hiddenness; they, too, are aspects of Ein Sof. In fact, they reveal perhaps the more essential aspect of the Divine Ein Sof; precisely because of their limitation and subservience to the laws of nature, they point to the infinite, which is beyond all law, whether of nature or philosophy.

Evidently, the Ein Sof is revealed both above and below. True, the lower revelation may seem to be a contradiction of Ein Sof itself, but it is only the apparent contradiction of opposites, the finite and the infinite. For it is this infinite, which is beyond all comprehension and form, that maintains the finite in all its forms.

We have here what may be called the paradox in the Kabbalah of the Ari. Since the unlimited is conceived as being beyond all things, and the sacred cannot be limited in any way, the very existence of the world is an insoluble riddle. And it does not matter whether the world is real or imaginary; even an imagined world cannot be resolved by saying that the Ein Sof is beyond all limits. From this point of view, the Divine, the more high and mighty He is, obligates Himself, in a certain sense, also to be closer than anything else to the reality of the world we recognize. Hence, the existence of matter, which is the other extreme of Divine hiddenness, is possible only by virtue of the power of the unlimited, which gives everything its existence. The existence of the world, by being dependent on the unlimited, requires that the unlimited should be confined to some limit; in other terms, since one cannot say that the Ein Sof is confined in any way, one has to presume that the Ein Sof, which is beyond all possible grasp, is the only basis for all these things that are graspable. The creation of a limit, or what is called the attribute of Malchut, the attribute of Divine concentration and withdrawal, is related in a very special way to the Infinite Ein Sof.

The existence of the world does not involve any change in

the self-sufficiency of God; creation is not a sort of addition or supplement to the Divine, even if the world may be seen as a sudden appearance of the limited out of the unlimited or of multiplicity out of unity. The paradox of God and the existence of the world may thus be resolved in many ways, but restricting ourselves to the statement that the limited is itself a manifestation of the Ein Sof, it may be said that there is no real new existence, but rather, as it has been said of the Torah, it is the play of God with Himself.

To be sure, any kind of illustration of this idea is grossly inadequate. Nevertheless, let us take the image of a person clasping his two hands together in a variety of positions. Each configuration of clasped hands is new and different and yet nothing has been added; it is always one's own same two hands. The world is thus a play of the two aspects of God—the "I am" who reveals Himself and the "I am" who conceals His countenance. But since both of them are parts of the same Ein Sof, the comparison of right and left hand may correspond to the attributes of Chesed and Gevurah, or the Holy One and "His Name." It is thus that the existence and the nonexistence of the limited world are both real aspects of the One who is limitless.

$$\sim\!\!\sim\!\!\sim\!\!\sim\!\!\sim$$

The power of speech consists of the use of certain symbols to transmit information of a specific character. It is not the information itself or the truth or the knowledge. Only the Divine is the knower, the known, and the knowledge all in one. Our words, concepts, and even thoughts are dependent on a certain limited "world"; they are restricted to the range of our senses and innumerable other factors. We cannot express much beyond it and, at best, we may be able to realize at times that there is something beyond the power of speech to express.

As for the power of the ear to hear, this too is a matter of the capacity to comprehend something. There are things one cannot express, perhaps, but that can be grasped emotionally or intuitively. But the union of the knower and the known is beyond even such a nonintellectual, intuitive understanding.

There are many things that may be considered a single entity from one point of view and a multiplicity from another point of view. This refers to anything, in fact, that can be taken apart into single units and includes most of the objects around us. In contrast, the unity of knowledge and the knower is not given to separation. When a person learns something, he embraces it and is embraced by it. This was explained by one of the disciples of Baal HaTanya by the image of two drops of water on the window sill. When they meet and merge, it is hard to say which drop absorbed the other; they become an indissoluble single larger drop of water that cannot be separated again into its previous components. Thus it is with the known and the knower, that which is contained and that which contains, the finite and the infinite.

Every day we learn something new, absorb additional information and knowledge. But it is not a simple adding of something to a storehouse; it is a complex process of integration. Knowledge influences the knower; the knower changes with what he learns. True, one may also forget what was known, but the impression made by the knowledge cannot be effaced. One can forget everything that one has learned, but one cannot wipe out the effect it had on the personality. Which, incidentally, explains why it is forbidden to put to shame a scholar who has lost his ability to remember. It is assumed that what he once knew remains as a subtle, ineradicable influence.

We have here a negative sort of definition: that which I can possibly understand is not the Divine. Which is in the nature of a warning to a whole category of persons, self-deluded by their common sense and logic into believing that they have achieved a certain grasp of what God is. Because God is that which cannot be grasped, and any claim to have done so can only be mistaken. It is like saying that one has grasped the horizon. To be sure, there are the biblical accounts of Moses and Isaiah or any of the prophets, but that is a matter of another kind of vision. Moreover, what Moses saw may have made him the humblest of men, but he was quite explicit in saying that man cannot see God and live.

Divine knowledge is not a matter of God's knowing more or less; it is all-inclusive because God is everywhere and there is never any time or place where He is not. He is within all existence.

The question is asked: Why, then, is it at all necessary to speak of Divine knowledge? And the answer – in this particular context – is that it is connected with the problem of Divine Providence and with Lower Unity. Although the world has no reality from the point of view of the infinitude, from the point of view of Lower Unity and the reality of existence, God is intimately connected with every particle of existence. Which brings us to a certain point of view, shared even by the Rambam, concerning the relation (of unity) between the knower, the known, and the knowledge. The Kabbalah does not restrict this unity to the Sefirah of Knowledge (Daat); it rather embraces all of the attributes. For it is not only a matter of Divine knowledge, of knowledge that belongs only to God, but of something that belongs to all of existence. It is existence that is full of the Divine essence. God, therefore, knows all our secrets, not only because God dismisses the fact that secrets exist, but because our secrets are an intrinsic part of us, and since there is nothing besides Him, His essence is in all of existence. He Himself is within us, within our being. So that what is being expressed here is not the universality of knowledge, but the all-embracing nature of existence, the fact that the Divine is in everything, and nothing can be apart from Him. It is not, in short, a matter of God and the world seen as a duality. They are one. God and the existence of the world, even as we see it, are inextricable.

In brief, God knows with the higher knowledge of "there is none besides Him" and with the lower knowledge of Divine unity, in which everything is filled with Him. He knows everything.

The ways of Divine knowledge are not at all graspable by man. And this, among other things, is what causes great suffering to man. We are born small, too small to express anything, and in the process of learning to express thoughts, we become overwhelmed by words, by the influence of environment and circumstances, so that we no longer distinguish the authentic. People learn to experience things as a result of outside forces, ideas, people, and so on. Historically speaking, we know that prior to the adoption of certain concepts, like that of a nation, for instance, people were unable to feel anything that corresponded to such categories. Many such notions, introduced from outside the reality of life, became an intrinsic part of the personality. The only knowledge of which a person can be said to be sure of is that of himself, simply, a knowledge of oneself, even if this is greatly obscured by the image projected by the world.

The Kabbalists felt that the Divine unity was valid for each of the ten Sefirot, that is to say: He was Chesed (Kindness, Benevolence) as an attribute, He was the one who gave Chesed and the one who was the object of Chesed; He was Tiferet (Beauty), the one who created it and the one who was affected by it, and so on. God was all the aspects of Divine manifestation; there was nothing in revelation that could be said to be out of the Divine; He was in all and all was in Him. Which is what is here called Lower Unity. It exists in the world below, in time and space. The Higher Unity defined by "there is nothing besides Him" is a nullification of all reality, which is the very opposite of the confirmation intrinsic to Lower Unity.

All of the above constituted, theoretically at least, one of the more outstanding differences between Chasidim and Mitnagdim. It seems there was a tendency on the part of certain thinkers of the time to speak of a gap between God and the world, as though the Divine had to withdraw from the world in order for Creation to take place. God was somewhere else, high up and distant. According to the Chasidim, this was a limiting of God, because it does not matter where one places Him, high or low, inside or outside; He is limited by not being everywhere. The argument, incidentally, deliberately uses the words of Maimonides's Thirteen Basic Principles. Because, to be sure, the argument is not against unbelievers; it is against good Jews, men of faith, who believe in Divine providence.

Since God knows everything and nothing can add to His knowledge, then the world below is united with the higher knowledge and with the upper spheres and is not separate. There is not, as many think, a difference between this world and a God who exists somewhere beyond in the transcendental. God is here, insofar as His knowledge and His Being are one. It cannot be said that this is true of man, of course, who can be in one place and think of something else, somewhere else. But in terms of the Divine, as said, there is no distance, no gap, between consciousness and existence.

God is thus at the same time that which encompasses all the worlds and that which fills all the worlds, the transcendent and the immanent. The four elements—earth, air, fire, and water—and all that these symbolize, are united only in Him. God is the basis for the reality of the world; He is Himself within all the particles of existence, from the largest to the smallest, and He is that which brings them together. Just as God's reality, His knowledge, and His creativity are one, so is His Providence, His all-seeing participation in the details of existence, impregnated with infinity and transcendence.

What is important to emphasize is the actuality of God in the world, that is to say, He is not beyond the world, and we have to relate to Him accordingly. To say that no one can grasp Him with the intelligence, no matter how superior, does not necessarily mean that human intelligence is limited, but rather that no one can grasp Him no matter with what means, intellectual or otherwise. In short, there are things that are not given to men to understand at all. In the same way, as stated elsewhere, it is not given to touch wisdom with the hands. It spills over into the absurd because there is no common denominator.

One can translate or transfer from one kind of being to another only when it is within the same realm of existence, whether material or spiritual. For instance, we measure heat with a thermometer that we read by the eye, or convert electric current into sound or light, by mechanical means. In the same way, we can translate various spiritual forms of expression in different ways—visual, audio, literary, and so on. What we cannot do is express anything that is beyond the spiritual. There is an essential barrier. Just as one cannot directly, materially, make contact with that which is spiritual. The essence of the Divine is, as was often explained, beyond the spiritual precisely as it is beyond the physical. That is, if one can say that God is spiritual because He is not material, then, in the same way, it can be said that He is material because He is not spiritual. Thus, no intelligence, no matter how great or spiritual, can grasp the essence of anything beyond the spiritual.

Nevertheless, God is the source, the Creator, of all experience, and something of His essence is contained in all that man does and thinks. But the presence of God in the world is not like the presence of the human soul within the body. This image, of God as the soul of the world, goes back to talmudic times, but is somewhat limited. Because for all the distance between soul and body, there is, nevertheless, a certain dependence that would limit the Divine. The soul does not only give life to the body; it also receives substance and the power to act from the body and is limited by its physical restrictions.

Indeed, if the soul could be so free of the body that neither pain nor pleasure could affect it, man would be much closer to Divinity. Just as the light of the sun falls on all things everywhere, the ugly as well as the beautiful, the dirty as well as the clean, and still the light is not made ugly or unclean. Because the relationship is one-sided; the earth receives the sunlight and does not affect it, whereas, the relationship between body and soul is a mutual, two-sided one. We cannot emerge very far from the restrictions imposed on us by the body, even when the intelligence uses the most abstract of thought forms.

In the story of Abraham's response to being told by God that he would have a son by Sarah, it says he laughed. And to the question, why did he laugh, the answer is given by the Maggid of Mezritch that, in spite of the greatness of Abraham's soul, it was still bound to a body and therefore greatly restricted, so that when informed of some kind of a release, Abraham laughed with joy.

The darkness and the light may be described as polar opposites, so that essentially they are part of a single whole. This is also true in the realm of morals, at least insofar as God is concerned. Darkness and light, good and evil, are all the same to Him. He is not made happy by someone performing a mitzvah, nor is He made sad by some transgression or other. People tend to believe that they are doing something for God by doing good, as though the Divine profits by it in some way or other, or that it gives Him pleasure. Whatever the difference, and there is a great one at many levels, between light and darkness, day and night, good and evil, it does not have the same meaning for God as for man.

For the truth of the matter is that God gives, but does not receive; He influences and is not influenced; He acts but is not acted upon. It is not a matter of the size or importance of anything, but rather of different worlds; God does not belong to anything knowable, nor can He be said even to exist in terms of the ordinary realm of things. For example: a person performs an act, good or bad. It can only be done with the cooperation of the Divine, because of the Divine force in him and the action of the laws of nature. Someone desecrates the Sabbath, let us say. It is done as part of, and within the framework of, a cosmos maintained by Divine power in all its details. All the laws continue to operate, unaffected by the person's breaking the Sabbath rule. God is oblivious. No matter how sincerely one endeavors to rebel against the Divine, God continues to give life and, altogether, is not in the least offended. To be sure, there may be reactions to such a rebellion as part of the laws of life and the world. What is more, a person can flourish even in sin, so that, it would seem, what we call the Divine indifference has moral implications.

Nevertheless, we do speak of the anger of God or of the fact that He is made joyful by something that happens in the world of men. Or as Rabbi Shimon Bar Yochai said about some unlucky person: "He acts thus and is hated by God, and I do not like him." This is the sort of statement that hints at more than it states. That which is not known definitely, but guessed at as a result of circumstances, is that a certain peron is "hated" by God—and this is meant in the same way, the same anthropomorphic image, as saying, for instance, that nature hates a vacuum. It is an image, and the meaning of it is simply that I don't like someone. It does not intend to convey a Divine sentiment. Nature, or God, does not love or hate anyone. When I say that God likes or dislikes a person, I am really describing the way this person relates to things of the world.

The anthropomorphic image, however, has its own necessity, its own emotional logic. When God is described as being furious with someone and binding the heavens with His wrath, the same forceful expressiveness cannot be achieved by an abstract statement to the effect that a Jew who falls into idolatry is opposing the inner, spiritual system of the universe and inviting disaster. Therefore, because of the limitations of the human soul and the human imagination, the writings of Scripture have to use anthropomorphic imagery. The distortion arises when modern man fails to respond even to this emotionally direct expression.

This is also perhaps what is meant by the distinction between God as "HaMemaleh Kol Almin" (He fills all the worlds) and "Sovev Kol Almin" (He encompasses all worlds). The former is the nearest thing to us, that which is ever present; the latter is transcendent and never to be grasped. The so-called contradiction between the two is explained by clarifying the difference between "Sechel" (Mind) and "Machshavah" (Thought). Mind is entirely spiritual and is a part of the powers of the soul. Thought is the particular action of the brain as a physical organ—it is integral to the outer personality, as are action and speech. True, thought is on the periphery of the material and in many cases may be considered spiritual. But essentially it is dependent on the mechanical powers of the brain, which can be damaged, and, just as injury to the mouth can impair speech, so too can the thought process be impaired. But this does not affect the mind that is the soul and that cannot be injured. However, the mind, which easily absorbs words of wisdom and does not directly relate to physical objects, can absorb the thought products of the physical brain.

One could say that thought embraces the subject; the thinker encompasses that which is thought about. So that if one thinks of the sun, the sun is thereby held within one's thought. Except that one does not really encompass the sun itself, of course. It is the mind that embraces a concept of the sun produced by the brain. Which is the difference between human thought and

Divine thought. Divine thought includes and encompasses the thing itself—because it is that which brings it into existence and constitutes its very life. The relationship of the Divine to all existing things is, therefore, very different from ours. What is more, when one's thought considers an object outside of oneself, it encompasses the concept and not the thing itself. Because the object is not in any way dependent on one. If, however, one creates a thought, or imagines something, then the image is indeed encompassed by the thinker and is totally dependent on him. Unlike the thought of something or someone outside, it is contained within the thinker. Thus, too, since the world is created by Divine thought, then the very existence of the world is one with Divine knowledge. His encompassing of the world is thus very different from that which is achieved by our minds. A human being knows something only from the outside; his knowledge is a connection between the human knower and the known object. To be sure, a created thought is perhaps more dependent on the thinker; it is an inner reality.

Thus, it may be said that the existence of the world is meaningful only by virtue of the fact that someone is aware of it. But since God is the ultimate truth, the world's existence is confirmed by His awareness and not mine. At the same time, this does not in itself prove the existence of God. We cannot grasp the reality of His Existence; it is a quality beyond us. And, of course, we cannot prove His existence by pointing to the world, which exists because of Him, or by the fact of our own existence in the world. The Divine is something on an entirely different dimension of reality.

The concept of "He encompasses all worlds" is a way of grasping Divinity as being aware of all that occurs in the world. And this includes all the details of all that takes place. Hence, we have what may appear a rather astonishing expression, that matter comes into existence from "He encompasses all worlds," which is spiritual in essence. The truth is that from the point of view of "He encompasses all worlds," that is, from the point of view that God creates the universe and the universe exists within Him, there is no difference between the material and the spiritual. To illustrate, let us conceive some objects such as a chair, an angel, and a man. From a certain standpoint there is no difference between them; they are all the same sort of thought substances in the mind. But what, indeed, is the difference? It lies in the details: What precisely is the nature and quality of each one? And this difference exists even in the realm of the mind: one is inert and the other is alive, one is spiritual and the other is physical. What is it, in other words, that constitutes the specific essence of that which gives existence to a specific thing, after we have accepted that all created things are equal in the mind?

Since all things, and even the sun, are limited, they are a contraction of the infinite. That is, every created thing gets its life-force and its being from a certain Divine essence that we call "He fills all worlds." But transcending all is that which we call "He encompasses all worlds," which also touches all things. Except that the latter does not go into details. To use a non-Jewish expression, it is the ground for all existences. And being the ground for all things, everything may be said to be within it, except that separate existences then have no meaning, no relationship. Whereas "He fills all worlds" provides the meaning and the specific relationship between each and every thing and between every thing and "He encompasses all worlds." Thus, it is not possible to speak of any severance between the Creator and the created thing, because there can be no existence to anything without the constant presence of the Creator.

In order for the created thing to exist, it must be limited and given its specific form. This means a certain contraction from the infinite to the particular, irrespective of size, even if a sun or a galaxy. All comes from the "breath of His mouth," and so an infinite number of worlds could just as easily have been created, each of them limitless in time and space. Without the act of Divine constraint, the world as we know it would not have come into existence.

Parenthetically, it may be added that God and His attributes are one, and there are infinite possibilities open to each attribute. Thus Chesed, for instance, can create a world in itself, in which case Chesed would be the content and the Divine Utterance the vessel that contains it, "like the snail whose garment is part of his body." Since the garment is not really an external article of clothing that is put on, but is part of the body itself, it may be said that the vessel and the content are really one. Thus, the Divine Utterance that creates the world can be a vessel of Divine Chesed. And since Chesed is infinite, God in His bounty could have created endless numbers of worlds, each of them unlimited in every way.

The question is asked: What kind of other creations can there be? Well, they are obviously other than the world we know, perhaps nonmaterial worlds. They may be less restricted, but as creations they have to be limited in some way. The restrictions can be of various kinds: Chesed has to be Chesed and not Gevurah, but a location need not be specific in terms of rigid coordinates of time and space. There are, for instance, many kinds of mathematical infinites even of different magnitudes and qualities, such as the number of points in a given line or the number of different kinds of geometrical forms. Even in our own real world, of course, there are infinite varieties and possibilities. So, too, in worlds beyond ours, there are creations with their own infinitudes and limitations, although our own world is considered to be the one with maximum limitations, the lowest world, in the same way that inert matter is lower than the human.

Another question is that concerning the "Sitra Achra" (the other side), or the realm of the demonic. To which the answer is that it is actually a part of this world. It is the lowest extremity of this world of our known reality. Were there an independent world of Sitra Achra, it would be beyond amendment and redemption. From the point of view of Divine manifestation, it is below the world of inert matter, although it remains part of our world. Evil, at all its levels, is still part of this world. Indeed, when we speak of our world we describe it as a world of both good and evil. Without the evil, our world would be very different, something like what is suggested by a description of the Messianic Age, or the World After Death, in neither of which does evil appear to exist.

Such a world, incidentally, would be a world without choice. Without evil, there is no choosing between right and wrong; at best it is a matter of choosing between two possibilities. Which, again, is a major question of principle: Can there be two equal possibilities? But this, in turn, hinges on the matter of Tzimtzum, of the Divine withdrawal. Thus, for example, the angel of death is built into the world—he is an integral part of it. So that it may be said that even at its best, our world has to have its framework, its limitations. The world is a picture in a frame, and the frame can also be viewed as the Klipot, the outer shell, or the peel of the fruit.

Hence, too, this problem of good and evil is really a matter of the outer shell. So long as the peel protects the fruit, all is well; it is only when one begins to eat the peel or the shell along with the fruit that something goes wrong. It is the mixing of good and evil that creates a reaction that is dangerous to the world. Evil distinguishes the good and the good can recognize evil; both can reside together in the world up to a certain point. The critical point of mutual tolerance is that point where light ceases to be visible. It is the same rule as that which defines a shadow. There has to be a certain minimum of light in order for a shadow to appear. Our world, it seems, is at such a critical level of tolerance; there is barely enough light for us to distinguish the darkness.

This relates to the question discussed elsewhere: What about the wicked who prosper? The answer is that the shadow points to light. At a level of evil completely without light or goodness, such a wicked person would not be able to exist. For the wicked to continue to exist, there has to be a certain minimum of a Divine spark present that maintains life. A completely evil person is something one may theoretically become, but it is not something that can endure for any length of time.

To return to the problem of Creation by Divine Word, the basic forces, in their inevitable breakdown into numerous forms, retain some indigenous element that repeats itself in a variety of transmutations, like the law of the conservation of energy. The Divine power remains the same through all possible development and alteration, even when the resemblance between the beginning of a process and the end is totally obliterated. Thus, it is said that one of the four aspects of the Divine Chariot has the face of an ox. This probably refers to some angelic being who certainly does not look like an ox or like any other earthly animal. The ox face seems to indicate something common to all the creatures of the earth, its outer form changing continuously. It is like the biblical expression in Genesis: "Let the earth give forth grass" (Genesis 1:11). This grass, which is but a single word, includes all the manifold kinds of plant life in the world from the fungus to the forest, all the vegetation that ever was and ever will be.

And all of these varieties of form have something in common, such as the fact that they draw on the same source. Similarly, the phrase, "And we will make man," manifests in the particular form of what a man is, and from this every human being takes shape in an endless variety of individual persons.

8

The Higher Sefirot

All the names of God, with which the men of the Middle Ages were so entranced, are really descriptions, or titles, that serve as explanations of the Divine. In terms of the Kabbalah, what is being considered are the various attributes of God, and the Sefirot are listed in hierarchical order beginning with His Will, which is identified with Keter. Following are ChaBaD, which are the three attributes of Chochmah (Wisdom), Binah (Understanding) and Daat (Knowledge). The next three are Chesed (Love, Kindness), Gevurah (Strength, Control) and Tiferet (Beauty, Mercy). And the last are: Netzach (Victory), Hod (Splendor), Yesod (Foundation), and Malchut (Kingdom).

Chesed is the act of giving—it is unlimited love and benevolence; Gevurah is the act of taking, restraining, or controlling, according to Divine understanding and by the use of Divine power, so that it results in Tiferet. Tiferet can be Rachamim or Mercy, Divine Pity, or it can be the Beautiful, emerging as a result of controlled and specifically directed abundance. The difference between the giving of Chesed and the giving of Tiferet or Rachamim is that when one gives out of mercy or pity, this is based on the fact that the other needs something that one wishes to provide, whereas Chesed is a giving that has no limit, that is, the limit is proportional to the measure of Chesed. Some may love more, others may love less. In Rachamim or Mercy, the measure is defined by the need, and it is in this sense that it becomes an act of splendor or beauty, that which is sometimes termed harmony; in certain places, it is called truth, and elsewhere it is known as the measure of the Torah. There is an objective quality about it that is not to be found in either Chesed or Gevurah. That is to say, whether one loves or whether one hates, one is hardly objective; the feeling is essentially drawn from within oneself and is relatively independent of the recipient. In contrast, Rachamim or Tiferet has to be based on an objective grasp of the situation; a feeling of compassion is directed toward something in particular. Thus, all the names or descriptions of God are Divine attributes, but they point to very specific aspects of reality.

The fact that man cannot get out of himself makes everything he does or thinks an extension of himself. For better or for worse, that is the way man conceives things and ideas. Where there is no physical, sensual basis, we make some picture of its effect on us and we form the world of the other accordingly. Man cannot have a mental grasp of anything except through the limited structure of the human mind. As Ibn Ezra said, the human soul conceives everything according to its own capacities, raising the inferior and lowering that which is above it. Anthropomorphism can function in two directions and can confer on lower creatures as well as on higher creatures all sorts of human qualities. Thus, in certain kinds of animal stories, the beasts and birds are made to feel and talk like people. It is the same kind of error, in a way, as describing the acts of angels or even God in a humanly comprehensible fashion. Thus, when one speaks of love, for example, it is considered to be the same kind of thing for animals, men, and angels.

To be sure, it is claimed that love is always subjective; there can be no other love but that which one feels oneself. In answer to which, let us presume that Chesed can be conceived theoretically as a certain kind of Divine attribute, a quality of attraction and benevolence that can assume a multitude of forms. But in one's own expression of this love, it is always very limited. Every creature experiences it differently, but it is the same paradigm, the same model.

Are we then bound to our own models? Can we not create new paradigms of experience? According to Baal HaTanya, we cannot, as was stated within a different context of thought. Thus, let us consider another Sefirah—like Keter (Crown)—the first of the Sefirot. It has no meaning for the human mind in its primary sense. It is too high, too abstract. So that we have to translate the concept of Keter as Will, which is something that can be grasped. And then, even though we are fully aware that this translation, or this image we now form in our minds, is not correct, we are unable to free ourselves of it. The range of our vocabulary and our thought processes is too restricted, and what is more, the mind always returns to its own patterns. One often observes how scientists, in attempting to explain unseen phenomena, will fall back on their own private realms of experience. We are limited by the fact that even ideas of vast proportions cannot be expressed except by ourselves. And all we can do is admit that the expression is not completely true, that it is woefully inadequate.

Anyone who needs models or metaphors for his work has often encountered the difficulty of being unable to extricate himself from the model and of going back to the original. The simplified sample has a hold over the mind that the complex source cannot always have. Indeed, everyone clings to a particular model of things, and this often serves as an obstacle to the truth of the matter. Of course, without these models it is virtually impossible to solve many problems. Indeed, in all the fields of human knowledge, we have the dilemma of the model that serves as an aid and becomes an obstacle to understanding. It may be likened to the previously discussed relationship between form and content, the inner and the outer, the light and the vessel to contain it. The light cannot exist without a vessel, it cannot manifest without something to reflect it, but when it does appear, one sees the object, the vessel, and not the light itself. The two have become one.

What is being explained here is the need for dependable points of departure. We define things, and our definitions certainly have a meaning. Nevertheless, they can get beyond the grasp of our intelligence. When one goes a little beyond the limits of one's powers of conceptualization, one no longer knows what one is talking about.

At the same time, we do choose one particular model rather than another, and no matter which we choose, the connection with the original concept is maintained. Thus, we make a model of the atom, for example, knowing full well that none of the relations are accurate and that neither the electron, nor any of the other particles, whether neutron or proton, are solid pieces of matter. Nevertheless, the model itself helps us to understand the atom so that it is possible to work on it. It is not at all a model in the sense of an exact reproduction on a different scale. It is a working model, an abstraction. The important thing is the inner relations between the parts.

In the same way, the human body is often used to express various metaphorical concepts. Thus, when we say that Chesed and Gevurah may be charted on a diagram of the Sefirot as right and left in terms of function, we do not mean to insinuate that Chesed is like the right hand of God or that it has anything to do with the right hand of a man. It is a model of only limited homologous relations that has value only because it enables the mind to grasp certain truths. Thus, too, many of the source incidents of the Halachah, as described in the Scriptures, are really only models. A butting ox, an exposed pit, and the like are models of legal problems or rather of relations between litigants. Unfortunately, too many of those who study Talmud find it hard to extricate themselves from the confines of the model. In this case, as in all instances of being trapped by the metaphor, the model becomes something absurd.

It is the imagination that interferes. One has to learn to function on two levels—one, recognizing that the model helps us to understand something, the other, that it doesn't really express the thing itself. This sort of intellectual difficulty is sometimes the chief obstacle in the way of certain cultures that seek to adapt themselves to a scientific approach. They confuse the model with the original object, often as a result of a long tradition of idolatry, of failing to distinguish the instruments of Divinity from Divinity. And the failure to free oneself from the model and to relate to the source is idolatry.

No matter, then, how much one praises God, He is still far beyond anything one can say or conceive, whether great or small. As far as created beings are concerned, the first attribute is Wisdom. It is the source. Nevertheless, it is with Daat (Knowledge) that the other attributes are most directly connected, and this is itself derived from Chochmah (Wisdom), so that love, fear, and so on need to "know" an object of their emotions, which also explains why children are often so angry and cruel—they do not have sufficient connection with Daat (Knowledge) and with Wisdom. Cruelty is, in most instances, a matter of not being able to grasp the essence of another creature, of not being able to put oneself in the place of another and to imagine his reaction.

The same thing is true of anger. Incidentally, Judaism never looked on children as innocent and pure. They were never considered little angels. On the contrary, they were considered liable to sin and cruelty out of ignorance. Man is not born human; he comes into the world as a wild young creature. As he grows, he may become tame. His wildness as a child is a result of not grasping the existence of the other; it is ignorance, a lack of knowledge, that makes empathy impossible.

Are we hereby accepting the principle of "natural" order, in which the big fish eat the little fish and everyone must fight for himself? To be sure, fish are not burdened with knowledge, whereas man does have some sort of knowledge of the other that is translatable as empathy and that repudiates anger and aggression. Cruelty, we say, is the result of ignorance, an ignorance of the other person, that is, and not an intellectual ignorance. Because a person can be very intelligent and lack knowledge of another person. There is even an expression to describe such a type: "A scholar without Daat," which is sadly appropriate for many of our intellectuals.

The idea here is that Knowledge and Wisdom have decisive influence over the other attributes. Thus, it follows, for example, that love cannot exist in the abstract. There has to be a certain amount of knowledge or conscious relation to something in order for love to manifest. There can be a great deal of attraction to something or someone, but this is not the same thing. All emotions and the attributes need Chochmah (Wisdom), Binah (Understanding), and Daat (Knowledge) in order to grow.

In fact, the three higher Sefirot, called from their initials, ChaBaD (Chochmah, Binah, and Daat), create the background for the existence of all the other attributes and their various activities. One loves or hates or pities, and this in turn stirs up thought processes that take form in words. To be more specific, there are two stages: one is that of the thought before it is expressed in words, and the other, when the thought enters into words and becomes indistinguishable from them.

The relation between thought, speech, and action is fairly clear and one leads mentally to another as, for instance, in giving an instruction. When it is an instruction given to oneself, as in operating according to plan, then the vessel is the body, and speech, or expressed ideas, is the soul. In terms of the holy letters, however, the letters of speech are the instruments, the body, while the letters of thought are the contents, or the soul, of the same thing. Ultimately, as mentioned, thought itself is also physical; it is a part and function of the brain and, therefore, of the body.

Insofar as the emotional attributes are concerned, like love and hate, words are not necessary at first. Only afterward are the emotions expressed in thoughts that act as the source for certain words. These words of thought, which are still far from being spoken, are what is called the letters of thought.

In other words, the "Sechel" or conscious intelligence constituting all of the three ChaBaD Sefirot, is the soul of all the other, the emotional, attributes, constituting the seven remaining Sefirot. ChaBaD can even be concentrated in the Sefirah of Wisdom alone as the source, so that wisdom can be considered the soul of all the rest of existence. "Sechel" or "ChaBaD" vivifies the other attributes, the various attributes vivify thought, thought vivifies speech, and speech vivifies action.

Now the essential point here is that there is no difference between the first Sefirah of wisdom and the last stage of action. Even though, for us humans, the distance between the two is the vastness of the whole spectrum of existence. This is all that we can possibly know, and the two are at the opposite ends. For God, however, the difference is of no consequence. What is for us a vast range of the spectrum of existence is for the Divine a mere speck of reality. It is we who have formed a scale of values, and there is no reason why it should bind God in any way.

9

The Secret of Faith

For man, wisdom may be considered the beginning of all things, but for God, Wisdom is a part of the completed action. The difference between the level of wisdom and the level of action is abysmal, including as it does the whole spectrum of human existence. But for God, this vast distance between wisdom and action is like a single rung in the ladder. To illustrate: the range of sounds heard by the human ear, from the lowest bass to the highest shriek, consists of no more than a few thousand wave lengths. And this includes the whole world of sound and music. But when this range is compared with the millions and billions of wavelengths that can and do exist in the universe, then there is no significant difference between the various sounds heard by human beings, and it may all be thrown together into a single category.

As it is written: "You have made them all with wisdom" (Psalm 104:24). God created with wisdom as His instrument, like man uses tools; wisdom may thus be seen here as something other than a Divine attribute—it can be considered a Divine tool. That is to say, wisdom is for God what action is for man. While for man there is a great latitude between the spiritual and intellectual influences and the physical and vital forces, for God there can be no such gap. Indeed, the gap for man is so great that it can be divided into five basic levels: Sechel (Higher Intellect), Midot (Higher Emotions), Thought, Speech, and Action.

Without entering into the complexity of these levels, we may note that they differ in three ways: in life-force, in quality, and in degree (grade or order). Thus, the life-force in action is as nothing in comparison with the vital force in the letters of speech, which in turn is quite insignificant in comparison with the letters of thought, which are, again, as nothing in relation to the higher emotions or the higher intelligence. Even more so is the difference apparent in terms of quality – that is, clarity or transparence – between the levels of being; the thought is clearer than the act, the soul is much more translucent than thought, and so on. And when one gets to the difference between the intellectual spheres (ChaBaD) and the lower attributes, the factor of degree becomes a matter of a distinctly other order of being, another plane of existence.

The space between the highest and the lowest of these extremes, between the spiritual and the most material, is as much as the human mind can cope with. We cannot proceed beyond them; they constitute the limits of our being. Beyond is the darkness at the end of the spectrum of visible light. Thus, when we wish to express the infinitely great, in comparison with which our whole world narrows down to a speck, we compress this entirety of our consciousness into a single entity and say that, for God, Wisdom, which is at the highest and the most abstract level, is equal to Action, the lowest we can perceive.

It is, therefore, not correct to describe God as "wise" or even to attribute wisdom to Him at any particular level. For wisdom as we know it is not of the same category as God's wisdom; it cannot transmit anything of the Divine essence. One cannot even say that it is difficult to understand Divine wisdom because it is far too sublime; indeed, such a statement is totally meaningless and irrelevant, like any attempt to determine something by means that have no reference to it, such as grasping a thought with the hands. "For the quality of intellectual comprehension in relation to God is considered as actual physical action."

Nevertheless, the Scriptures do call God wise and good, and so on. And, after all, we cannot very well maintain that He is so far beyond us that we are unable to relate to Him and to His wisdom at all. The truth may be said to lie in the fact that He is the source of wisdom; God is the first cause, the basis of all creation, and from whatever we comprehend of creation we call Him wise. Similarly, we call Him merciful and kind and so on, because He is the source of all these attributes. These attributes describe God's actions and not God Himself, in the same way that we describe Him as "He who gathers the winds and brings the rain" (daily prayer book) and do not thereby identify Him with wind and rain.

The manner in which the Divine forces of God are emanated to take form as wisdom in the World of Emanation, and how the various levels of being are made to emerge one from the other, and the relations between them—all this belongs to the teachings of the Kabbalah. Since we are not able to enter into the intricacies of this ancient lore in this discussion, we shall suffice with the observation that God and His attributes are one. That is, the Divine Will, Wisdom, Understanding, and Knowledge are one with His Essence and Being.

Evading thus the details of the mystery of God's withdrawal and contraction in order to create the world, we are nevertheless compelled to face that which is given to us to know, the twin aspects of faith. The first is that God's Essence and Being are above and beyond all that we can possibly grasp; the second is that God is revealed to us through the higher Sefirot in such a manner that there is a unity between each Sefirah in its capacity as instrument or channel and the Divine essence operating at that particular level. In a certain unaccountable way, the Sefirah serves not only as an external instrument for the Divine essence, but at the same time as an expression, a revelation, of Divine existence itself.

But even the way that this expression occurs is as much beyond us as is God Himself. The most we can say is that in spite of our inability to grasp the real quality and greatness of the Sefirot, we at least have some idea of what we are talking about. Clearly, we do not grasp wisdom at its higher level, but since we do know what wisdom is at our own level, we have something to clutch at. Because there is a certain correspondence between the Sefirot of the World of Emanation and our own inner world. Our souls are a sort of copy of the World of Emanation. For this reason, we are able to relate to the Sefirot in spite of the difference in level between us, which, incidentally, is not only a difference of quantity but primarily of quality. Notwithstanding, and despite the fact that the Wisdom of Emanation is not like our wisdom and Divine mercy is far from the mercy we practice, we can relate our intelligence to the truth of Divine wisdom and we can try to purify our hearts to approach whatever we conceive to be the Divine attribute of Mercy. For evidently there is a correlation, if only because we clearly distinguish between wisdom and folly, between compassion and cruelty. What is more, besides the fact that the attributes are distinct and separate one from the other, there is also a very profound and dynamic inner relation between them all. And this, too, we know from the most intimate knowledge we possess of ourselves.

The Sefirot thus offer us a means of defining the wisdom of God for ourselves while admitting that the Divine Essence is forever beyond us. And indeed, because of our limitations, we cannot relate the Sefirot, even the highest Sefirot, back to God's Essence and Being. We can, however, say that He is united with His attributes inwardly as well as externally, and that the Sefirot can be illuminated from within, so to speak, by His light. In this way Chesed (Loving-kindness) is not at all external, like a hammer in the hands of the worker; it is rather like something that is acting as an instrument for an entity from which it cannot be separated, just as the limb of the body or the body itself cannot be totally separated from the will behind it; the hand that acts is "transparent" to the soul that is expressing itself through it. In a manner of speaking, therefore, the Sefirot are instruments for whatever Divine forces are "making use" of them. That is about all we can be sure about; we are still in ignorance about the essence of the Divine Himself, as said, so that this certainty to which we cling concerning the unity of God and the Ten Sefirot is really a matter of faith.

Consequently, these Divine attributes, known to us as the

Ten Sefirot, are called in the *Zohar* "the secrets of faith, which is the faith that transcends intellect." After all, it is faith that provides the meeting point with those realities that baffle us. And of such an order is the connection of the Ten Sefirot with God. All we can say on the basis of the "secret of faith" is that God gives the Sefirot their form, and that He acts in them and through them.

In the foregoing, we have dealt with the sublimity of the godhead and its implications. In a roundabout way, our analysis has led us beyond the clear abstractions suggested by the Rambam about the incomprehensibility of God, that He is the Knower, the Known and the Knowledge. True, this conception certainly fulfills the demands of the absolute otherness of the Divine and makes it impossible for the intellect to come any closer. But in our discussion, besides confirming this absolute sublimity and infinite otherness of God, we have made use of the Kabbalistic teachings to assert the existence of an opening for a more human relationship to God. This opening is provided by faith in the revelation of God through the Ten Sefirot, which, with all their loftiness, can be directly related to the reality of our human existence.

10

The Sefirot and the Days of Creation

he Torah speaks "the language of man" in order for man to understand it in such a way that he is at least able to relate to it with the ordering of his life (if not with his mind). It is also the primordial design, the archetypal metaphor whose origin is God Himself. From this point of view, the giving of the Torah is like God's gift of Himself to man. It may be regarded as the permeation of the inconceivably great into the circumscribed domain of the human. But the only way for men to comprehend it is through allegory and metaphor. By such means, the human mind can make leaps and build bridges to overcome the abyss in some pragmatic way. This has been done by the "scholars of Truth," the sages of the Kabbalah.

For example: These scholars of Truth have called the Sefirot "lights" to help us understand the nature of the unity of God and His attributes. For actually, the distance between God and the Divine attributes is too great for us to cross; all our ordinary comparisons and standards are woefully inadequate. Moreover, in the higher worlds, the essence of all things is so much greater and more varied than anything we can conceive, and the difference between levels of existence so much more

108

pronounced that we cannot consider even the possibility of a relationship that can overcome the vastness of the gap. All that we can have any idea about, as said, is based on the Secret of Faith, on the premise that, in a manner we cannot fathom, God does unite with the Sefirot and acts through them. And since permission has been granted to speak of the Sefirot by the use of allegory and metaphor, we are able to obtain a certain insight into the relations between the human and the Divine in the world.

To return to our Kabbalistic example of calling the Sefirot "lights," the metaphorical image is that of the light of the sun and sun itself. Before it goes forth from the globe of the sun, the light is an inextinguishable part of the sun and has neither name nor existence. Only when it is separated from its source does this radiation become something in itself, identifiable as sunlight. As it is written, "And God called the light—day" (Genesis 1:5). This metaphor (of sun and sunlight) has already appeared in our dissertation, but whereas previously it was intended to portray the nullification of creaturely existence in the Creator, here the intention is to show the unity of the Sefirot with God. It is appropriate only in that it helps to see the relation between the Sefirot and their Divine source and to illustrate how the "Secret of Faith," although it transcends reason, can be grasped by the mind.

To pursue the image further, just as the light of the sun becomes visible to us only upon separating from the sun, so too do the Sefirot exist for us only when they issue from the World of Emanation. Before that, they are still united in the one Divine reality. (But, it must be repeated, the image is inadequate; no words or metaphors can do more than express our limitedness, to "enable the ear to hear what it can understand.") The Sefirot are emanated and assume their separate identities to our consciousness; at the same time we are contained in them and guided by them.

Just as Genesis is a creation of a world out of nothing, so too are the Ten Sefirot called forth out of God to direct hidden worlds and revealed worlds, for as it is said in the Introduction to *Tikunei Zohar*: "You conceal yourself in them." God clothes Himself in the Sefirot in order to sustain the world He has created and to control its course. And since it is in the nature of a garment to both reveal and to hide, so too do the Sefirot reveal God's action and conceal it. Through our dim cognition of the Sefirot, we become aware of the way God directs us and our world.

Thus on the first day of Creation, the attribute of Chesed (Grace, Loving-kindness) was revealed. This is in accordance with the Kabbalistic view that each of the seven days of Genesis marked the manifestation of another of the lower Sefirot, and on the first day it was Chesed. To be sure, all of the Sefirot are manifested in every process or phenomenon, and therefore they would all be present on the first day. This is what is known as "Partzuf" (Countenance), the whole experience in which each of the Sefirot contributes its feature to comprise a living face. Moreover, since each of the Sefirot includes all of the others, the attribute (Sefirah) of Chesed, which is the special revelation of the first day of Creation, is Chesed as a generality, including the other Sefirot in various combinations: Keter (Will), Chochmah (Wisdom), Binah (Understanding), Daat (Knowledge), and so on.

With Chesed He created the light through the utterance, "Let there be light" (Genesis 1:3). And the light was diffused from one end of the world to the other. Which spreading and diffusion and revealing of light streaming around and into all of reality is the attribute of Chesed. Because, as we may readily observe, the light of the first day is not the light of the sun (which was created only on the fourth day). Chesed, the "light of seven days," is another sort of light; it is a light that suffuses the whole of creation without limit, from one end of the world to the other.

However, as we have said, the attribute of Chesed does not manifest in its purity on the first day as that which is only Chesed; it comprises something of the other Sefirot as well, in particular the attribute of Gevurah. This attribute of contraction and the restriction of force and substance within limits is absolutely necessary for Chesed, which knows no such limits. If Chesed were to try to manifest pure and infinite in its power of giving, it would not be able to be "clothed in" (operating through) this world, which is finite and everywhere confined in its physicality. Therefore, too, the light of the first day is not spiritual in the absolute sense, like the supernal light; it has to be able to establish connections with this world. This is possible through the action of the second attribute of Gevurah within Chesed itself.

"In like manner, on the second day of Creation, the attribute of Gevurah was revealed." Here, too, since all of the Sefirot are included in each of the Sefirot, Strength too was not manifested in its purity, in its Almighty power; it necessarily had to include Chesed (Loving-kindness) and various combinations of the other Sefirot. And with this was created the firmament with the Divine utterance, "Let there be a firmament in the midst of the waters and let it divide the waters from the waters" (Genesis 1:6). The action of Gevurah was to separate and divide and fix limits. And the creation of a firmament was not only a matter of fixing a radius for the sky, a parting of the waters above and below. It was the act of primordial division between the higher and the lower, with the firmament acting as a sort of fixed frontier in the created universe between the spiritual creatures of the heavens (upper waters) and the material creatures of the earth (lower waters). The "lower waters" are the primordial stuff out of which all the substantial things below are made, the earth and all that is on it, whereas the "upper waters" above the firmament are the essence and the source of all the spiritual things, at all their very many levels. The creation of the firmament is thus the establishment of the original barrier between the spiritual and the material, between "above" and "below."

This division is obviously not just a formal one of categories—it is a division that determines the very essence of all things—because in fixing the spiritual as a separate entity and the material as another entity, the effect is to sensitize the spiritual and to coarsen the material. Since all material substance is set into a world of its own, in an environment that is physical and dense, it tends to become ever more inert and unresponsive. The same is true of the spiritual in the opposite direction—it tends to become rarer and more refined in its own higher realm.

However, as said, Gevurah does not manifest as a single,

pure attribute with sharp limitations; it has to contain something of the attribute of Chesed at least, for the world is built with Chesed (Psalm 89:3). The resolute action of forming a barrier between the upper and the lower worlds is actually a necessary step in the process of creating the earth, its physicality and fertility, its ability to give birth to new forms, new life. It is from the earth that man was created and it is from the earth that man draws sustenance to exist and to fulfil the purpose for which he was formed. The Gevurah that is the chief manifestation of the second day thus has within itself also Chesed and the other Sefirot needed to break out of changelessness and rigidity and to establish the groundwork for "Chesed to build the world." At the same time, of course, there is a clear distinction between the first day and the second day, between the gracious giving without stint and the defining of boundaries to this benevolence; the second is needed in order for everything to find its place, the material to the material, the spiritual to the spiritual. The formation of the elemental barrier between upper and lower worlds is indeed primary; from this moment it becomes virtually impossible to cross over from one to the other.

Similarly for all the other seven days of Creation and the Sefirah characteristic of each, what happens is a combination of forces that makes for a living and creatively dynamic reality. Thus the third day is in the sign of Tiferet (Splendor, Harmony, Mercy), which is the attribute blending its two predecessors, Chesed and Gevurah. It has the advantage of both of these, the wideness of the sea and the charm of place on the land; it expresses both the harmony of their multiplicity in Creation and the vigorousness that is necessary for individual growth. As it is said in *Tikunei Zohar*: "Tiferet shows how the world is conducted with righteousness and justice, (for) righteousness is law, justice is mercy." Both law and mercy are required for social justice and the ordering of human relations. Indeed, Chesed of itself, the act of love and of giving without limit, could prove disastrous if it is not controlled by duly considering the needs of the receiver. And this consideration is essentially compassion or mercy, the attribute of Tiferet. After all, justice is not merely the exacting of punishment or the passing of a verdict; it is also a matter of weighing all the factors involved, balancing the mitigating evidence, and so on. For the sin itself is beyond correction, at least as far as the act is concerned, and only the consequences can be related to. In such manner, true judgment comes to direct the course of the sentence. For law only distinguishes between good and evil, right and wrong; judgment is the proper use of mercy.

This substantiates the truth that the purpose of the Sefirot is not only to conduct the affairs of the world but also to help the world. To be sure, the human values we somehow transfer to the Divine attributes are very different from their actual meaning, so that what we consider to be just from our point of view may not be the same as the Divine Tiferet and what we feel to be merciful may not be quite the same as what God intended. Nevertheless, we are convinced that God acts with justice and mercy in everything, even when we cannot understand it on any level. The point is that we cannot grasp the attributes on any other level but our own; the explanations we give are not able to define God's real Essence and Being. It is simply that through them He measures us; they are the mode by which God makes all things happen in the limited reality within which we exist and to which we respond.

11

Thought and Speech

It has been mentioned that all the expressions we use concerning Divinity are relative and derivative, and can be traced to our specific place in the world. Expressions like "the hand of God" have no independent meaning, nor does "Divine Mercy" or any other of our descriptive phrases. We have to use words, of course, but we have to realize their limitations, and the anthropomorphic tendency, which, in this context, makes all language questionable. Thus, when we speak of the Ten Utterances (that created the world), we do little more than denote the place of each aspect of existence in the Divine hierarchy and its relation to the others. We also learn the way all things, all forces, are related, even if only by analogy. True, the likeness between certain ideas and forms may sometimes be very superficial, but they serve to enhance our understanding of a particular thing. Thus, when we speak of the Utterances of God, we do not, of course, mean to imply that God makes certain sounds, but rather that the infinitive "to say" or "to utter" designates a specific relationship, a form of communication, a transfer of meaning from one dimension to another. In the phrase, "God said," we are trying to explain that He transmitted some meaningful communication from a higher level to a lower level. And since we have to use images, we tend to use the human soul as our metaphor.

We can thus presume to state that Divine attributes are revealed as qualities in men and are manifested, to begin with, as primary impulses. Through humanity they act on the world, which is on a much lower level. But they come already clothed in the letters of thought. Thus, the impulse to be kind comes from the attribute of Chesed, which is a much wider and more inclusive force, a thrust of Divine grace, of emergence from confinement. Humanly speaking, the impulse of kindness has to become specific and defined by thought in order to be projected into action; it has to become a qualified act of giving something to someone in order to be meaningful. One cannot act without some degree or other of consciousness (thought), and this is expressed more intensely by breaking the thought up into words and into its "letters," that is, into its basic components. Because most thoughts cannot be put entirely into words. At best, they are put into words or language at a later stage, after they have assumed some sort of existence as a separate impulse, as the "letters" of thought.

Of course, one does not think in terms of written letters. Thoughts are formed as conceptual entities and these can be considered "letters" or building blocks of language. If I like someone and want to do him a kindness, there is first this feeling of love and the impulse to do something about it, to give something, and then comes the thought about the performance of the action in its details. There are people who reflect about something endlessly, turning it over in their minds again and again in the transmutation from impulse to action. Even those who claim to act without thinking, totally on impulse, may be observed, on closer analysis, to go through three, four, or several stages of development, or whatever is needed for the thrust to take form, from raw impulse to language, to doing.

Of course, there are situations when the transition from letters of thought to speech is more direct—as in command or in expression of a feeling. The point being made is that there is a necessary gap between thought and speech, between the attribute, or impulse, and the action.

However, all assumes meaning only when some sort of

communication takes place. Thought is a transfer of something from one level to another within the self; speech is a transfer of something particular in oneself to something that is in the category of "another." Therefore, when we say that God had a certain thought, or that He spoke, we have to see it as an outer manifestation of something in God to that which is other than God. To be sure, these are only operative descriptions; they do not really define what Divine thought or Divine speech is.

The letters of the utterance of God are the smallest fragments of the communication; they are necessary for the flow of action. What is being said, to repeat, is that a Divine attribute is far too big and broad a province for any single human being to be effectively influenced by it. It has to be broken down into the details and fit the specific requirements of a situation. Love, for instance, cannot be expressed in its vastness and power. It has to be narrowed down and given form, distinctiveness, quality, and direction. In other words, love has to be communicated in its "letters" and their combinations in order to be effective. Words are one of the intermediaries, flowing from attribute to action, covering much of the gap between the general and the specific.

For instance, in order for Chesed to create light, a transformation of Divine power has to take place from the vast inclusiveness of Love to a specific thing, like light—just as any other acts of Chesed, whether it is the unthinking act of handing a child a piece of candy or nullification of one's self, have to be defined in order for them to manifest. In order to create light and not any other thing, the utterance has to assume its word formation, "Let there be light." But unlike human communication, this utterance it not directd to someone else. It is a combination of letters, and every letter is a specific manifestation. The purpose of the utterance is to make finite and concrete that which would otherwise remain infinite and abstract.

Thus, even though light is one expression of Chesed and water is another, they are obviously not the same thing. The whole question of difference between one thing and another may be explained, at least partially, by the example of the decimal system of numbers. The first ten numbers may be

likened to the chief categories of reality, and the figures after a
decimal point may be considered the identification mark of
each substance or quality – the more the figures, the greater the
accuracy.

Even light is a general entity, for there are many kinds of
light. To create light, a certain amount of qualification has to
accompany the commandment, and these qualifications are
implicit in the letters of utterance "Let there be Light!" It is a
sort of extremely complicated Divine code. Every letter and
vowel and emphasis in the Torah is a level of communication.
But, of course, like all complex form or color, it cannot be
defined precisely by number alone. There is a matter of
position, quality, and the like. The utterance as a whole has its
own force, its own destiny and effect. So that when it does
communicate with reality in this world, it manifests as light –
after going through other worlds, other realities, where perhaps the manifestation of the same utterance takes a different
form – just as, within the physical framework of our world,
light can be transmitted as electromagnetic rays, as electrical
impulses, or whatever technology can devise.

The important thing, then, is the original message. At the
source of the Divine utterance there are neither written letters
nor expressions of any kind; it begins as a far more inclusive
force that finds its appropriate manifestation at every phase,
giving it ever more particularity. It is like visually recognizing a
letter according to its form, then bringing it to a mental
identification and a sensing of its sound effect, and finally
placing it into a context of words and thoughts.

This transfer of a Divine impulse from one level of reality to
another is our guide for study of Torah. One carries something
from one system to another. Thus, study of Torah can be confined to a single detail, or it can be broad and universal, according to the degree of carry-over from one system to another.
In its widest sense, the study of Torah is a re-enactment of
Creation, a transfer of primal force from one system to another.
The change of form is only an apparent, and often a rather
strange, side-effect of this transfer – like our surprise at the basic
connection between color, sound, and tone.

Everything that exists has to be recreated anew every moment. The process is described as a flow of life-force from His will, which is Keter, the highest Sefirah, and from His wisdom, otherwise known as the Father, through the seven attributes, the seven days of creation. Two kinds of worlds are thus formed: hidden worlds and revealed worlds. The difference between them is like the difference between thought and speech: one is concealed from outside, and the other, overt. Because thought is not simply a flow of mental energy in the brain, it is an inclusive and hidden action of all the parts of the body and the whole of the being. And the difference between thought and speech is not merely a matter of the operation of different organs (the brain, the mouth, and so on). So that if speech can be said to belong to the mouth and action to the hand, writing can be called a form of speech; it is speech with the hand. And when a person talks aloud to himself, he is really thinking.

One of the ways of grasping biblical prophecy is to think of the prophet as someone who listens to God's talking to Himself. Thus, like the first Divine utterances, "Let there be light," "Let there be a firmament," and so on, God's speech is intended to be made manifest outwardly, and the prophet is the one who, after a fashion, hears it and passes it on, so that it becomes manifest, whereas that which is not heard, becomes the hidden world. This is the world that is not projected outward. When a person thinks and reflects creatively, that which is created is an inner reality that remains hidden, although there are ways of projecting it outward, thereby making it a part of the revealed world.

All of creation is a product of Divine speech. What is this power of speech? Human speech may be described, technically at least, as certain movements of sound waves induced by physiological means. Divine speech is certainly not connected with sound waves or anything of the sort, or even with what we would call spiritual forces, because, as said, Divine Creation includes everything, the spiritual as well as the physical realms of being. So that Divine speech is above anything we can conceive; it is His very self emanating and offering itself to that which is outside of Himself. Even in human speech we may distinguish something of this. There is a speaking that is over and beyond the grasp of another person.

And, indeed, every real teaching process is of this kind, a giving of more than is already known and understood, so that the receiver has to open himself to a new level of thought. Speech is thus something that is possible on very many levels, beyond even that of the human. And when we try to grasp the essence of Divine speech, we are conscious of something beyond man addressed to man, to which we can only give the name: The Word.

The Word is a combination of many definite forces, and its utterance is a release of something new, a creation of light or firmament, or a special fin on a little fish swimming in the sea. The general Word–Light, or Sea, or Creatures of the Sea–has to be brought down to its infinitesimal details. In this way are all the worlds filled with created things–physical, mental, spiritual, and so on. According to the wisdom of the Chariot, there is an archangel responsible for each and every kind of creation, an archetype that contains the root and the essence of a certain plant, animal, or thing. Indeed, prophetic vision is sometimes reputed to be the capacity to identify such an archetype or essence.

There is the biblical description of one of the prophet Jeremiah's first visionary experiences. "What do you see?" God asks. And Jeremiah answers: "I see a rod of an almond tree." He responds very specifically about what he sees; it may have been something very different, something of a spiritual quality, like the angel Gabriel. But the rod of the almond tree was the nearest to the message being conveyed, and the prophet's task was to find the words to express it. The same thing is true of all that is manifest. Each thing has a particularity that is part of a definite general category. This is in contrast to the Sefirot, which in themselves are general and infinite in their scope.

Not only can the letters of Divine speech create a world; they can also create Man, who contains in himself all the levels of intellectual attainment. So that these letters of Divine speech are far beyond anything conceivable by human thought. One can hardly compare Divine speech and human speech. Nevertheless, there is something we can learn: The physicality of human speech is based on the breath. This fundamental breath, still unsounded by any other tonal effort of the body, is usually depicted as the first letter, *alef*, a letter without any substance, as was said by the Ari. Hence, too, the expression—with *alef* the world was created. This breath, or silent nothingness, is the driving force behind all the other letters of speech, which are formed, phonetically, by certain controls or Tzimtzumim (constrictions) of the breath by the lips, mouth, tongue, larynx, and so on.

From this, it may be gathered that the life soul of the first man, which includes the whole range of human experience, is formed by the fundamental, still unsounded breath syllable, that which precedes speech. To depict it is, of course, beyond human intelligence, even when this reaches the very great heights and levels of knowledge in such persons as Tzadikim who, it is said, are superior to the angels. In other words, this primordial Divine syllable contains the souls of all men, including those of the prophets, like Moses, who spoke with God. To reiterate, then, Divine speech is something of another order; it is called speech only because of the transmission of creative force that is involved, from God outward. Hence, too, the name "letters" or signs, in Hebrew.

The world was created by Ten Utterances. And our error is in trying to understand this as ten statements, or so many letters, words, and so on. Whereas as we have already explained, the phrase is a way of expressing something beyond comprehension, a certain revelatory action of God, which we interpret as utterance only because of its analogous function to human speech that serves to reveal what is being thought.

Thus, the twenty-two letters of the Hebrew alphabet are projections or symbols of basic elemental units of creation. Every letter stands for something different, a revelation, a certain force. They are not the same as Divine attributes or Sefirot. The letters are specific forces that are much more limited, more defined. Unlike Chesed or Gevurah and other attributes, which are difficult to define, emotional in nature and infinite in scope, the forces of the letters are like the forces of gravity, or electrodynamics, with relatively fixed characteristics that can be formulated. This is only a metaphorical way of explaining it.

Alef, for instance, stands for an objectless force, something not confined to any one aspect of being, unlike the other letters, each of which has a fairly definite character. Indeed, there are a number of profound writings on the subject of the letters and their physical form as part of their metaphysical meaning. Some letters, like *shin*, are more inclined to incompleteness; others, like *yod* and *vav*, are more basic; *heh* is a *dalet* with a *vav* or a *yod* added. There are places where the *heh* in the name of God is written differently from other places in the text. One can begin to understand the symbolism of the letters by recalling that in chemistry, too, the letters of chemical formulae for certain substances have a variety of meanings depending on the weight and place of the letter. The letter expresses a specific element or substance that has no "meaning" in itself, even though it can be either useful or harmful within a certain context. In other words, it has qualities that give it uniqueness, but they are not the same as the attributes of the Sefirot, which are fundamental, archetypal, and without limit.

The letters are thus elements for making various combinations expressing certain functions; they are not the same as the Sefirot. That is to say, the division of the Sefirot into ten separate entities does not really affect the letters because they are part of a different structure. Nonetheless, there are points of contact.

The letters are emblems for definite tendencies and forces, as well as numerical values; the Sefirot indicate very general basic powers and qualitative realms of being. A force in nature, as symbolized by a letter, does not possess a character and it is limited in its power to act, whereas a Sefirah is itself the essence of the character, and there is no limit to its scope of action. To be sure, there are instances when one of the letters of a certain word (usually one of the names of God) stands for a specific Sefirah.

In contrast to numbers, which are only signs of quantity and can be written any which way, the letters of the alphabet are meaningful also in their physical form, so that the slightest alteration in the structure of a letter can have immense implications. There is a whole range of levels of meanings to each of the letters. In the Talmud, for example, it is said that once the children learning to read used to make puns, saying that the *gimel* is the one who bestows (*gomel*) Chesed, and *dalet* is the poor (*dal*) one; and although *dalet* doesn't ask for favors from *gimel* out of shame, nevertheless he reaches out a little bit, a hand, a finger stretched forth, and *gimel* sets forth a foot because that is his task, to pursue *dalet* and give him what he needs to give. Also, *kuf* is holy (*kadosh*), and *resh* is the bad one (*rasha*). So that *resh* does not face the *kuf;* he turns the other way, away from the holy, for that is the nature of evil. To be sure, there are many profound analyses of the meanings of each of the letters. One of the more recent ones is the little book by Harav Kook, *Rosh Milim.*

To sum up, just as the letters of human speech are projections of the mind, so are the letters of Divine speech projections of great elemental forces of being.

12

Creation is Always New

T he word is created from letters and these letters combine in various ways, but the word itself is more that a combination of letters. It has its own meaning, which is greater than the letters and which dominates the letters. The play of letters is, therefore, not a simple thing. In chemistry, one can play with the letters of a formula, and though it may sometimes be interesting in itself, it only has meaning in terms of material substance and chemical reaction. In the Kabbalah there can also be a play with the letters of a word or a text. But it, too, has meaning only in relation to physical or spiritual reality. Thus, it is not actually a play with letters that is involved, but a play with certain forces. To be sure, one can also learn something from the play of letters, but this is still not a creative act, although there is a connection. Moreover, as we can conclude from the perils of irresponsible playing with chemicals and chemical formulae, there is a very serious and profound aspect to the play of letters and words— whether or not we admit their symbolic or their direct power.

"As for example, through the words of the utterance 'Let there be a firmament,' the seven heavens and all the celestial hosts were created." From which it is evident that there are seven firmaments. Admittedly, the frontiers of these firmaments are not at all clear, because each of the firmaments is itself a realm besides dividing one species of reality from another. Moreover, anything that so separates is also a medium or vehicle of communication between one kind of existence and another. That is to say, each of the firmaments has its own heavens above it.

Then, quoting the talmudic passage (*Hagigah* 12b), some of these firmaments are pointed out. One is called "Shechakim," which in Hebrew also means to grind or to beat fine, because of the millstones that grind out manna for the Tzadikim. Manna is the essence of food, the purest kind of nourishment, indicating that these heavens serve as a mediating factor between the spiritual world and the need of the saints on earth for sustenance. "Zevul" is that firmament that corresponds to the heavenly Jerusalem and the Holy Temple and the Altar. As it is written: "Lord of the Universe, You have built for Yourself a Holy Temple on earth corresponding to the Holy Temple in the Heavens." All that is and was in the Jerusalem below expresses the essence of the Kabbalistic notion that the world below is an attempt to copy the world above. The world above is, of course, of another kind, and all that the world below can do is emulate the forms and images to furnish some sort of habitation for the spirit.

The firmament known as "Machon" contains the snow and the hail. And the others of the seven firmaments also act as mediating levels between the upper and the lower worlds. To be more precise, they act as plateaus serving to break the force of that which streams down from above, enabling it to undergo a certain crystallization or actualization.

To be sure, the heavens are not locations made up of perceptible areas as much as they are different realms, layers upon layers, firmaments upon firmaments of great variety. There is one that acts only as a curtain, opening and closing all the time, yet forming a screen or a partition, between one thing and another. It has no other function.

To return, then, to the problem of Divine speech, we see that the utterance is a whole in itself, not merely a combination of letters. And every letter is meaningful in a new way because of the meaning of the words and of the utterance as a whole. So that the same letter in a different context will have a different significance, even though it may have the same form and structure. Thus, the letters of the utterance "Let there be a firmament" belong only to this utterance and create the detailed parts of the firmaments.

Even the same combinations of letters do not express the same things in different contexts. Every new combination is the true name of a given creation. So that every created thing has its own particular name, composed of letters and integrated into a larger context specific and unique to itself. As was mentioned previously, every child has his own true name, which the parents try to hit upon when the child is born; but if they fail, then the child will keep on searching and changing his name until the true name is discovered. Incidentally, it is written in some books that every person has two names—the name of the sanctified self and the name of the outer shell—and that the name of the outer shell should not be known by any man, it being the name of one's other side, the unholy aspect of personality.

To illustrate the importance of the order of letters in a name, it is said that since antecedent letters dominate, the first letter is primary and the following ones succeed in diminishing order of importance. What is more, there are certain combinations of letters that are units in themselves, that are not meant to be taken apart, such as, for example, the first letters of the Divine name, *yod* and *heh*, which frequently form parts of proper names of people like Yehoshua, Eliyahu, and Yehudah.

Of course, the letters do have a phonetic meaning in terms of language and as such reappear in numerous ways, in multiple combinations. What is being said here is that the letters should not be understood only as parts of the alphabet; they are elementary forces, and it is as primal forces that they combine and separate in various ways. There is the primary level of creation and there are succeeding levels of particularization, of breakdown into details, each one with a different combination of letters and each one further from the source.

The letters receive their light from a Divine source, and yet keep changing constantly in meaning and luminosity in the same way that the moon and the earth itself reflect back the light from the sun according to their changing positions. This merely testifies to the principle of the relation between the primary light and the secondary light source. It is not only a matter of quantity of light; it is also a matter of quality. The nature of the light changes upon being reflected from the moon. The whole matter, therefore, of the transition, the Tzimtzum (contraction) of the things of creation, involves a change of essence from Divine source to actual being. Nothing can actually come into any sort of contact with the primal light. We are always experiencing only the light from the moon, so to speak, so that we are like night creatures who sleep during the day and do not even know that there is a sun. If one were to try and explain to such a creature that the moonlight was really coming from another, a greater, orb of the heavens, his words would not meet with much conviction.

This brings us back to the problems of the Creation in terms of the formation of being, Life in terms of one's ability to act and to know, and the cosmos in terms of existence as a continuous phenomenon. We began with the recognition of the fact that the existence of the world as a whole is not an independent thing; it is what it is because God speaks all the time and maintains it with the Ten Utterances. The sky exists because He says "Let there be a firmament," and so on. Thus, too, God's word creates the light, the heavens and the earth, creatures and man, constantly.

The Baal Shem Tov, reflecting on the verse in the Psalms (119:89), said that the Word is still there, upholding the sky. This found stirring echoes in the minds of his disciples. The same comment is found in a midrashic exegesis on the Psalms written a thousand years before. But it is not the same thing as that which was spoken by the Baal Shem Tov. Because it depends on how and in what context a thing is said; that which was said by the Baal Shem Tov had another meaning than the same words spoken by different persons on different occasions.

Thus, since it is God's word that creates the world, the process begins with an utterance that has to be projected through all four worlds, Emanation, Creation, Formation, and Action. Above us, then, are creatures far beyond our comprehension. We cannot imagine the nature of these upper worlds and all the created forces they contain, like angels, seraphs, and the like. The descent of the same letter or word proceeds in a series of contractions of light until it creates the lowest level of the stones and dust. The difference is not only of essence, between the holy and that which is not conscious; it is also between that which can rise in consciousness and that which can never lift itself up. There is, in this respect, a level even lower than stones and dust; it is the level of a man who does not wish to rise. As it was said, "I am a worm, and not a man"—it may happen that a man can be worse off than a worm. A worm has limited form, it is bound by Divine will and performs the Divine will completely, and it cannot deny the Divine as men are prone to do.

We see, then, that the descent of a particular combination of letters from layer to layer of worlds eventually creates a particular stone or a particle of dust. Everything has its name, so to speak, its Divinely apportioned existence. If the word of God does not speak in it, it can no longer be what it is; and this is what is called the soul of a thing and the working of Divine providence. All proceeds from the creative utterances of God that continue to divide up and project themselves in manifold languages and substances and combinations, descending from level to level, remaining always the Word of God, speaking and acting and creating all that exists. Within such a universe, each creature, each particle, has to be in its proper time and place.

This concludes the work we have been studying called *Shaar HaYichud VeHaEmunah* (Gate to Unity and Faith). The book began with an introduction concerning matters that every Jew should know, such as the existence of levels of knowledge of the Divine and the meaning of the love and the fear of God. Within such knowledge, there is something that is fundamental, something called "the education of a child according to his own way so that when he grows old he will not depart from it." There has to be a basic structure from which a man does not depart, through all the rises and falls in life. And there have to be falls in life, especially when there is progress, because in moving up from one level to another, a person often loses his balance, unable as he is to be in both levels at once.

The danger of this fall between two levels is the inability afterward to find one's way again. The meaning of the saying, "A Tzadik shall fall seven times and rise" is that being a Tzadik is a risky affair, full of disasters. An ordinary, unsaintly person will fall relatively less because he keeps going in a more or less even course without many problems. The Tzadik is always aware of an anguish of mind and soul, a heartache that is part of his sainthood. In this connection, there are many stories about Noah and Abraham, each of whom was a Tzadik in his generation. The idea of many of these stories is that at another stage of his eternal life, in another generation, the saint may have been something completely different, such as an unmitigated evildoer. For in passing from one stage to another, the perils are so enormous that he is bound to fall some time or another.

Consequently, the advice given in "Gate to Unity and Faith" is intended to serve as a support for a man in the passage from one stage to the next. When a person proceeds from the depths to the heights, he needs something to hold on to, although, to be sure, knowledge is useful at all times, not only in times of stress or danger of falling.

Nevertheless, the book is not a general outline of the fundamentals of faith. It is a treatise on one particular aspect, not adequately explained in other works, namely the constant presence of God in the world and His relation to the Creation. The author does not deal with the act of Creation itself, with Genesis or the origins of things. For him the important thing is the living connection between creatures and God, and the need to take this out of the realm of past history and to make it a present reality. God did not merely create the world in the beginning; He creates the world constantly by His speech, and the only one who can answer Him is man. All the other creatures in the world are merely products of the Divine utterance; only man can respond to God.

The world is being created at every moment. This makes it

possible for man to create himself, because that which existed two minutes ago is a different world. Now a new world has been formed and there are new people and new situations, and one can create one's own world anew.

This optimistic spirit is parallel to another statement to the effect that no man struggles all his life between good and evil. He struggles for only one moment at each conjuncture, at each choice. The decision is always now, at the moment itself. And there can be no other moment of struggle and choice that is exactly like this present one, in which I create a world. Every moment is unique. And once the world thus created is manifested, it becomes a part of the infinite reality of multiple worlds. In one such world, I can be a Tzadik; in another, a moment later, I can be something else entirely.

In short, the question is always being asked of one: "What are you doing at this moment?" It is in this sense that God creates the world and the only one who can answer is man. The other creatures of the world are part of the Divine speech; man can also respond. God can say: "Let there be light!" and man can say: "I don't want it," or he can say: "Hear O Israel."